# The Toilet Paper Principle

A Funny Little Book About the Overlooked Human Side of Incident Response

Eric Olson

# Dedication

For my friend Anna, this book would not exist without your lollipop moment, and for my IR younglings, Andy and Elvis, Neeraj and Jasmine and Chris. If our really bad day ever comes, I hope I will lead you well. This book is for you.

# Contents

# Introduction: The Toilet Paper Principle

One August morning, longer ago than I would care to admit, I woke up in a little apartment in Washington, DC, where I had arrived just 12 hours earlier. I showered, dressed and walked, full of vim and vigor, to my first day of Business School.

Back then, Georgetown's Operations Management class was taught by a Professor from South America named Ricardo. Ricardo had decades of Ops experience. He'd consulted to some of the biggest manufacturing companies in the world about operating in tough places. He'd learned the hard way how to keep things running under difficult conditions. Professionally speaking, the guy was a total badass.

When he walked into the room, it turned out he was also so astonishingly handsome that the women in the class instantly took to calling him Ricky Ricardo. For those of you old enough to remember who that is, you know what I'm saying. For those who aren't, just Google "Desi Arnaz" and accept that, in his day, he was a big deal.

Ricardo glided through the door in a powder blue shirt and black slacks, slender and poised, with the grace of a flamenco dancer. A hundred pairs of eyes looked on. A hundred pens poised over a hundred notebooks. A hundred of us leaned forward with bated breath, eager to capture whatever wisdom awaited us.

And Ricardo? Ricardo made no introduction. He just stood there, still and striking, taking in the impossibly attentive faces. Then, without preamble, he reached into his briefcase and took out, of all things, a roll of toilet paper.

Holding it up in one manicured hand, he said in his oh-so-romantic accent, "Let me ask you something." He even sounded like Ricky Ricardo. "How much is this worth?" Then he tossed it into the front row. A bit perplexed, we passed it around. We muttered about prices where each of us had come from. We studied the roll of toilet paper in case there was something special about it. There wasn't.

At the Professor's urging, a few of us called out our best answer. Some said fifty cents. Some thought half that. Back and forth we went until the roll made its way around the room and ultimately back to Mr. Movie Star with his rolling R's and his dazzling smile. Holding it up once more, he summarized. "OK, consensus estimate, fifty cents?"

The hand went down. The roll went back in the briefcase. "Good," he said. "Fifty cents." In the next moment, he somehow managed to look all one hundred of us dead in the eye at the same time, and then he said this.

"Not. When. You need it."

So this is both the origin and the wisdom of The Toilet Paper Principle. Though this wasn't his point at the time, I think it's pretty much the best summary I've ever heard for how to think about Incident Response. The day you need it is *not* the day to figure it out.

Some of you reading this might think there is no shortage of books, courses or (ugh) compliance frameworks that discuss how to "do" Incident Response. I agree. Want to analyze malware? Take a disc image? Parse a firewall log? You've got your pick of a hundred books on Amazon. The world doesn't need another one, certainly not one written by me.

Despite twenty-five somewhat accidental years in cyber security, in my heart of hearts, I'm still the MBA bean-counting weenie that Georgetown made me. I'm a business guy first and a security guy second. (I am also, as you will see, from New York and as such moderately but incurably profane. Sorry.)

But that's why I think this IR book *is* different. Besides the profanity I mean. What *this* book is about is the stuff that those technical books and compliance frameworks and SANS courses gloss over, forget, or never thought about in the first place. *This* book is about the underappreciated aspects, the behavioral and organizational challenges, the psychological burdens, and ultimately the very human job of leading *people* through some of the toughest days of their chosen career.

I also want to say up front that the words may be mine, but this isn't just, or even mostly, based on my own IR experience. Rather, it is a distillation from interviewing roughly two dozen experts with well over 100 years of cyber experience between them. When I first took over management of IR in a Fortune 500 company, I really wanted to not screw it up. I thought I understood the technical stuff well enough(ish), but I'd never had to *lead* people through a major Incident. So by email and Slack, Teams calls and text messages, I kept asking the same question:

*"Like every large company, we've got policies, plans and tools. But Incident Response is also about people; the Responders, the executives, the lawyers, the victims. In your experience, what's the stuff that's overlooked? What's the stuff you had to learn the hard way? If I end up having to lead through a major Incident, help me learn the human-being stuff that's not in the manual."*

Then I furiously scribbled down everything they shared. I guess in the end you could say that when I set out to write "a funny little book about Incident Response" I did it largely by doing the same thing I did to get through Ricardo's class many years ago. I shrieked for help, then copied all the homework from people smarter than I am.

I don't presume that every admonition or key learning here will strike you as wisdom for the ages. That said, I probably learned a hundred useful things I didn't appreciate before I asked, and I figure if you take away even a handful that are truly valuable to you, then I will have done a good deed.

By distilling the experience of the wise and the battle-worn, perhaps I can help you respond just a little faster, incur a little less damage, and recover with a little more agility and grace than you otherwise might. Most of all, my wish is that while doing all those things, these hard-won lessons will help you be there for the people who have committed with all their talent, skill and heart to be there for you on the days you will need them most.

# Part I

# Before the Storm

# 1.
# Saber-Toothed Tigers

> *"Stress is not a state of mind... it's a condition that reduces the ability of your brain to function properly."*
>
> – Gabor Mate

Like so many cyber security writers before me, I'd like to begin by talking about giant man-eating cats.

As I mentioned in the Introduction, this book is mostly about how and why to do a variety of things that aren't in the usual technical guides and training courses. The underlying reason for a great many of these overlooked topics is actually rooted in this first underlying and ultimately *non*-technical challenge.

This first and most-essential thing we need to cover is the brain science of Incident Response, or rather the brain science of people under stress. Please trust me when I say we have to talk about this before we talk about any of the other stuff. And when I say "brain" science, I am going to start more specifically with one little peanut-sized gland in the center of your head. It has ensured that our species survived for all of history before the modern age. That peanut, the amygdala, plays a lead role in interpreting the signals being sent to our brains by our senses and evaluating them for imminent danger.

Sort of like an endpoint security agent screening endless activity on a PC, it mostly sits around being pretty chill. It's constantly assessing the bajillions of things our senses ship off to our heads every second of the day, including the 99% of those stimuli we don't consciously process. For example, I'm currently listening to music, but until I thought about it, I was utterly unaware of the other auditory inputs in my environment like the sound of the dishwasher in the next room.

Now suppose, like a suspicious unknown script launching on my laptop, that my brain were to process among all the other noises the low growl of a wolf at the patio door. Well then the "Detection" module would go ding, and the "Response" module would kick off an entire cascade of crazy things in my brain and body. We collectively summarize these reactions as the "fight or flight" response.

This response protocol evolved to keep us alive in what I'll call acute circumstances like, say, being chased by something with big pointy teeth that wants to eat you. Being designed for such time-sensitive issues as staying not-eaten, the system evolved to operate over a duration that might encompass, let us say, seeing a giant, man-eating cat running toward you and then either successfully climbing a tree or, y'know…not.

In other words, win or lose, it's a system that was built to run for minutes at a time. It was never intended to keep you going at 150% of sustainable intensity for days or weeks or months. That single fact, that first-of-all-things, is actually the underpinning of a great many of the overlooked aspects I learned from those wiser peers about leading people through a long-haul Incident.

As you may know, a lot of what the fight-or-flight system does is pretty widely understood. Blood flow and respiration spike so you can run, kick and bite at the top of your game. Adrenaline and cortisol flood the bloodstream, improving agility and reaction times. Your pupils dilate to let in more light so you can see better, increasing the chances that even at a dead run you will spot that one low-hanging tree branch. Your body even makes your sweat extra stinky. No kidding, "fear sweat" is actually a thing. Being stinky increases, however slightly, the chance that whatever growling thing bites you will decide you don't taste very good and will spit you out in favor of antelope tartare.

This whole system was here long before our prefrontal cortex, that analytical, logic-following, pinnacle of human evolution. Back then, using more than a vowel made you the Shakespeare of your day, and analysis consisted of deep insights like "green fruit bad, red fruit good." In those days, the amygdala was pretty much the reason for your survival.

Experiencing actual Shakespeare and red fruit fermented into Merlot is all thanks to the later arrival of our big ol' prefrontal cortex. But the tiny gland that allowed us to survive long enough to enjoy both? It has no notion of, or capacity for, high-falutin' fanciness like language or logic. We are, in biological terms, a hot minute from the knuckle-draggers running from saber-toothed tigers. So when that little sucker grabs the reins, all those poetic, wine-sniffing higher functions of modernity go right out the window. Ditto by the way for your memory, analytical skills, and attention to detail.

This has a number of important implications for Incident Responders, and for managing those Responders when the crap hits the fan. A colleague I interviewed for this book has one of the craziest resumes I've ever encountered. He has been, among other things, the owner of an IR firm, the CISO of a cryptocurrency bank, a startup CEO, an instrument-rated pilot, and a beat-walking police officer. In other words, he knows a thing or two about staying cool under many kinds of pressure. He told me this.

"At the police academy, when we were training for a high stress situation," he says, "like a fire fight or a door knock on a dangerous fugitive, the instructors gave us this advice. When things go sideways, the vast majority of people do not in fact 'rise to the occasion.' They sink to the level of their training."

I love this so much I can't even tell you.

The relevance of this insight for both the Responders and the people who lead them are why I began the book with this topic. Under stress, the ability to analyze data, to process complex information, or even to understand language declines dramatically. Your lizard brain responds the same way to the roar of a tiger, the boom of a gun, or the progressive destruction of your Azure environment, because that part of your brain can't tell them apart. It just knows it's in freakout mode. In that moment, training, documentation and process are what people will, indeed what people *must*, be able to fall back on.

The rest of this book is not really about the technical processes or steps housed in those documents, training sessions or exercises. That's the stuff that *is* covered in the standard manuals and training courses. What the rest of this book is about is how and why to get those things right.

My own IR team is so young, so bright, so passionate. I adore them. The chapters that follow are just my way to try and share what others have shared with me, so that together we can do our best to lead people well and care for them when the chips are down.

# 2.
# Get Your Docs in a Row

On to the exciting topic of... documentation. Most IR training manuals do have some element along the lines of "you should have an Incident Response Plan and here's what should be in it." I wholly agree, and as I've said, I'm not here to regurgitate the stuff that's in the usual courses and textbooks. I just think they often miss the bigger picture.

I believe there are four, yes four, levels of documentation you and/or your providers need to have. I may not actually succeed here at making this topic exciting or anything, but I hope at least you will see that they're all good to have. The docs in this case are Incident Response *Policies*, *Plans*, *Processes* and *Procedures*. I'm going to talk for just a minute about what each one is, with a quick example at each level of detail.

An Incident Response *Policy* exists to establish and document the organization's commitment to detecting and responding to cyber Incidents. It should define high-level responsibilities, explicitly assign authority and accountability, and specify regulatory and compliance requirements. It should *not* provide detailed steps or specific workflows for handling Incidents. Likewise, it should *not* name specific vendors, tools or systems.

"And why is that?" I hear you ask. Because *Policy* documents are not only reviewed by, but often submitted to and kept on file by, auditors and/or government regulators. This matters because the process of version control, submission, receipt confirmation, review and so on is therefore tedious, labor-intensive, and costly. My point? Policies are necessary, but keep them as general as you can to minimize the amount of churn and labor you have to invest in upkeep. (Also, if the regulators themselves are breached, you don't want *your* detailed IR plans to be a bonus prize given over to the thieves. Defenses will get analyzed, named parties will get spear-phished and so on.)

The purpose of an Incident Response *Plan*, by contrast, is to outline actionable steps and roles for responding to Incidents. It should include response phases, communication paths, and escalation protocols. It applies equally to various types of Incidents. It does not specify granular, task-level actions or step-by-step commands but it says, in essence, "you know all that stuff we claim that we do in the Policy document? Yeah, we should be able to show that when we said, 'Our company is committed to doing this important thing' we actually have a high-level Plan to, you know, do that thing." IR Plans are for people who manage Incidents.

Compare this to *Processes*. Processes are for people who actually *respond* to Incidents. Process documentation provides structured workflows, and a specified series of steps for handling different categories of Incidents. It should standardize the sequence of key tasks for each to ensure consistent handling. It does not dictate tool-specific instructions or individual clicks on a mouse.

*Procedures* by contrast *do* dictate tool-specific instructions and individual actions. This is the most granular level. Its purpose is to give step-by-step instructions for dealing with a specific type of investigation, down to system commands and data entry. Think of Procedures as, "Oh, you're the new guy? OK, when we say 'isolate that host via the EDR console' we mean do this. Exactly this. Exactly as shown in the screenshots on page 3."

This may feel a bit abstract, so let's illustrate by example.

One sometimes-sticky wicket in Incident Response or cyber investigations is exactly how far the IR team can and should invade the privacy and/or surveil the activity of a User. In my experience, in the absence of "probable cause" as it were, companies are pretty reticent about climbing into your digital knickers and rooting around without a reason.

By contrast, in the *presence* of such probable cause, e.g. once some tool or tip line has given me a reason to get all up in yer drawers, the gloves are pretty much off. So on this point, a ***Policy*** level document might go something like this.

> "*When informed of a potential Incident as defined in the Incident Response Plan, the cyber team is authorized to monitor relevant IT resources, retrieve communications, and access other relevant records without notice or further approval.*

In other words, the Policy says the IR folks have the right to do certain things when necessary. At the ***Plan*** level, this might be specified in a bit more detail, along with specific do's and don'ts.

> *"Upon identification of a potential Incident by manual report or automated control, the IR Team is authorized to access and monitor relevant IT systems and User activity, including logins, communications and browsing activity to identify unauthorized access, system misuse, theft of company resources or violations of company policies."*

> *When undertaking such activities, the IR team will notify the CISO or their designee that such actions have begun. In addition, a log of all such monitoring will be maintained, and a summary report will be generated after each Investigation."*

So the Policy level document says that you're authorized to do a thing under certain circumstances, while the Plan level document says, "Hey, if you actually do that thing, there's a couple of boxes you need to check and some records you need to keep."

The ***Process*** level goes a step further, defining specific steps by which the directives outlined in the Plan are satisfied. It might go something like this.

> *Step 1: When a potential Incident has been identified by tip line, automated alert or other detective control, the Incident Responder should verify the scope of data access (e.g., system logs, session records, communications) needed for investigation."*

> *"Step 2: The IR team shall notify the CISO and, as appropriate, members of the IT and Compliance teams regarding any access requests, logs, or surveillance actions required to conduct the investigation. The Incident Commander or designee shall maintain a record of all data requested or accessed and relevant findings identified."*

*"Step 3: Once the investigation is complete, the IR team will prepare a written after-action report, which will include a section documenting access or surveillance activities undertaken during the process, as well as specifying the underlying rationale for those actions. Any confirmatory or exculpatory findings shall be noted."*

That's a simplistic example of how Process documentation might differ from the ones above. It should not be confused with ***Procedures***, which are the granular, detailed, step-by-step instructions for the brand new analyst who actually has to *do* the work. Keeping with this same example, that might look something like this.

*Procedure for Accessing Browser Activity for Incident Investigation"*

*How to retrieve User Browser History:*

- *Look up the endpoint in question via the EDR console. See screenshot below.*
- *Pull down the menu on the right that says "Actions" and select "transfer files."*
- *When given a prompt, paste the file path below, edited for the name of the browser (e.g. Edge, Chrome etc.) in the sample file path. <path>*
- *Save the file returned to the secure folder created for the Incident in the IR team's SharePoint site at e.g. IR_Team_Data/Browsers/<IncidentID>.*
- *Log this action in the case notes at location Incident_Audit_Log_<IncidentID>.txt*
- *Review the logs and document findings as outlined in the IR Process handbook.*

In a small shop, you might argue to combine the Process and Procedures, and that's a good discussion to have. Either way, this chapter was by no means intended to describe in detail what needs to be in all those documents at all four levels of detail.

Rather, my hope is to just show their differences and why each one of these four levels of docs is important. Each has a role to play in serving the ultimate goal, which is to help you handle a major Incident with speed and consistency should you need to, even when your brain is in tiger-evasion mode and not thinking all that well.

So having said all that, it may surprise you to learn that I'm now going to start the next chapter by telling you this; The Plan I just advocated for? Yeah. Worthless.

Read on…

# 3.
# General Wisdom

*"Plans are worthless, but planning is essential."*
– General Dwight Eisenhower

You might think I am contradicting myself from the pages you just read by starting this chapter with the adage from Ike that plans are worthless. I'm not. Let's break this down.

Even though "plans are worthless" I stand by my point of a moment ago that it is vital that you have one. I think what the General really meant was that it is vital to go through the exercise of *creating* the plan. The document itself is not the objective, since, by his own admission, it may well be inadequate to the reality when the time comes. But the effort to prepare the plan will require familiarizing yourself with your own resources and assets, your defensive posture, the terrain, and how and where you *think* the enemy is likely to attack.

So the plan may be worthless but you should go through the planning process anyway. Make an Incident Response Plan, and make sure it *does* include at least all the stuff that *is* in the textbook or NIST Standards or whatever framework you're using as a guide. A surprising number of companies below the Fortune 500, and/or those not in industries where this is required and audited by regulators, don't fulfill this most basic of requirements. Have. A frickin'. Plan.

So let's assume you've done this and now you do indeed have a capital-p Plan. To quote another often-cited General who fought his way across Europe, Helmut von Moltke famously said, "No plan survives first contact with the enemy." (Or as Mike Tyson so eloquently updated it for our age, "Everybody's got a plan 'til I punch them in the face.")

Like the American who would later follow in both his philosophical and geographical footsteps, I do not believe the Prussian General was arguing against having a plan. On the contrary, I believe he was arguing for the importance of having thought through as much as you can ahead of time, since if you count on nothing else, you can rest assured that whatever happens, it won't be what you expected.

So consult the Policy document that outlines your commitments and priorities and prepare your Incident Response Plan accordingly. This is not because it will properly prepare you for what will happen when the battle is joined. It won't. What makes responding to a major Incident so complicated is that it never goes down the way you expect. If it did, it wouldn't *be* a major Incident, it would be a garden-variety nothingburger. But without a ready-made plan that handles at least some parts and pieces that *do* match expectations, then literally everything is a scramble, a mystery, an utterly unwelcome what-the-hell-do-we-do-now.

In essence, your Policy drives your Plan. Together, these two are the conjoined twins of *what* you will do when things go wrong. They're the more high-level half of all that stuff you'll need to keep everyone marching in the right direction when the cyber bullets start flying, and everyone's brains go all fuzzy. Properly preparing for *how* you'll do those things are the downstream half of the preparation-and–documentation framework for which I am advocating. Let's take a closer look at that second half, those processes and procedures, for just another minute so I can try to show you just how big a difference they can make.

# 4.
# Green Fruit Bad, Red Fruit Good: The Power of Procedure

*"Under conditions of complexity, checklists are not only a help, they are required for success."*

– Dr. Atul Gawandi

So here's a thing about me. I'm a pilot and an aviation buff. Like every aviation buff, I have a favorite airplane. In my case it's the Boeing B-17, which many historians credit with a larger role in the outcome of WWII than any other single aircraft type.

The first B-17 was created in response to a US government competition for a new heavy bomber. The prototype, Boeing Model 299, was bigger, faster, better armed, and carried a larger bomb load than its competition. It was also an engineering marvel for its day, and a strikingly beautiful airplane to boot. It flew higher, farther and faster than anything before it, and it bristled with so many machine guns that a reporter who first saw it dubbed it a "Flying Fortress." The press was wowed. The Generals were giddy. The public was in awe.

Boeing lost that competition to the B-18 Bolo. The B-18 was a slow, ugly, pot-bellied sow of an airplane that was so bad, even the people buying it hated it. Why did the B-18 win? Because on October 30th, 1935 the B-17 prototype crashed just prior to the final award, technically disqualifying Boeing from winning the initial contract.

An investigation quickly found the cause of the crash, which was as straightforward as it was tragic. The flight crew had neglected to properly release the gust locks. Gust locks are metal pins that prevent the control surfaces like the rudder or elevator from getting banged around by high winds when the plane is parked. With the pins still in place, 299 was unable to control pitch properly. She nosed up, stalled and face-planted into the ground.

Fast-forward sixty years. I first learned to fly in a Diamond DA-20. The DA-20 is basically the motorized version of an Austrian glider. It's made of composite materials instead of metal. It weighs less than a large horse. If you walk out to the flight line and plunk your butt down in a DA-20, there are forty-four checklist items to complete before you turn the key. Not before you take off. Not before you taxi to the runway. There are forty-four items to complete on the checklist before you *turn the key*. On what is basically a toy airplane.

The prototype of a war machine that brought Nazi Germany to its knees? A hundred foot wingspan, a crew of ten and 30 tons when loaded with high-explosives? Yeah. No checklist.

This is the lasting legacy of Boeing 299. The Inquiry concluded that this four-engined behemoth was simply too complicated a machine for anyone to operate from memory, which up to that moment, had been the standard, indeed the only, method. As a direct result of this accident, the so-called "to check" list or "check list" (later one word) was developed.

While this story is well known among pilots, it was brought to a much larger reading public in a best-selling 2009 book by Dr. Atul Gawandi called The Checklist Manifesto. Gawandi is a surgeon who was educated at Stanford, Oxford *and* Harvard and is therefore clearly stupid. In his book, he utterly demolishes the notion that even the most successful and exquisitely trained experts, a category that includes himself, can or ever should rely on experience and memory to do things right when it matters most.

Now in the majority of cases, cyber Incident Response may not be a life-and-death thing, though depending on the impacted systems it could be. A really bad Incident could certainly mean life or death for the targeted company, though. So let's talk about the power of writing stuff down in high-stakes professions, as illustrated with a few examples from Gawandi's book.

Consider this one first. In a direct causal line from that B-17 crash in 1935 to the religious use of checklists in aviation today, your current odds of being killed on a scheduled passenger airline flight are in the range of one in 15,000,000. (To put that in context, you are twelve times more likely to be *struck by lightning* in a given year than to die in a commercial airplane crash.)

Similarly, thanks to the less publicized but equally rigorous use of checklists in the construction industry, of the buildings built in the United States each year, the odds of one suffering a structural failure due to human error is about one in 53,000.

Here's another stat you'll find interesting for comparison. In 2009 when Gawandi penned The Checklist Manifesto, *if* you happened to be one of the 150,000 Americans who either died or suffered a severe complication each year during a surgical procedure, your odds of being dead or nearly so because of an avoidable human error were one in… two.

Read that again.

In the US at that time, of the Americans who died or had a serious medical problem *caused* by having surgery, *half* were the result of an avoidable screw-up. To see what the humble checklist can do for this highest-of-stakes kind of problem, consider this. A pilot program, (see what I did there? in a chapter about airplanes?) using a small-scale test across ICU's in the state of Michigan resulted in a two-thirds reduction in post-surgical infection rates.

What did that abstract fraction mean in the real world? It meant *$175 million* in cost savings and an estimated 1,500 fewer dead people. In a small scale trial. In one state. As the author states, a well-made checklist is incredibly powerful in "combating failures in attention, memory or thoroughness."

Remember like five minutes ago in Chapter 1 when we talked about what happens to your brain under stress? I think there was a bit in there along the lines of "something something stuff that goes right out the window such as attention, memory and thoroughness."

Hopefully the applicability to Incident Response is self-evident. I just spent Chapter 2 arguing that IR Policies may be no fun, but they are necessary. In Chapter 3, I explained that IR Plans may be "worthless" but they are necessary. Well, Dr. Gawandi makes a more compelling argument than I ever could that, even more than those other things, written *Processes* and *Procedures* are absolutely necessary. So grab a pen and a clipboard, and start checking boxes.

One last thing. A nuance that my interviews indicated a decent percentage of companies miss. When I say "grab a pen and start checking boxes" that's not metaphorical. It is apparently not uncommon for all the knowledge needed during an Incident to be stored in a folder or a share drive somewhere on the company network. It can get kind of awkward if you can't work an Incident using all those processes you so diligently created because the network where they are stored happens to be the thing taken out of action by the attack.

Every single one of your critical processes and procedures needs to be on paper, in a binder somewhere. Even if you need to do it with a pen, start working down your checklists. It might just help you avoid a crash.

# 5.
# The List by the Phone

In my house growing up, like all my friends' houses, there was a phone hanging on the kitchen wall. It had one of those corkscrew-spirally self-tangling cords that seemed to contract into a gordian knot during the wee hours of the night when there was no one there to catch it in the act.

Like all my friends' houses, next to the phone, stuck to the wall with tape or pinned to the fridge with a magnet or hanging from a clipboard, was a list of important numbers. In our case it was the Delaneys next door. The pediatrician. Uncle Tony and Aunt Vivian. Frank Girardi, the plumber who would fix a toilet or a furnace on a Friday night without charging a crazy premium. Y'know, the critical few.

And like all my friends' houses, stuck to the back of the handset, or stuck to the clipboard, or on the piece of paper itself, was a green Mr. Yuk sticker with the number for the Poison Hotline. (Note to self - since the demise of landline phones, do more kids die from drinking bleach and eating paint? I should check on that.)

Now obviously if Mom or Dad were home and needed to reach someone important, they wouldn't need the list. They had all the important phone numbers memorized. Yes, that used to be a thing. People did that.

But suppose there was someone else left in charge. Let's say, for the sake of argument, it was me or my brother or a seemingly-but-not-actually-responsible babysitter. And let's say, also just for the sake of argument, aforementioned someone needed to get hold of one of those critical people right-freakin-now because another someone just ate a bleach-and-paint sandwich.

Every single parent who ever put a Mr. Yuk sticker by the phone understood that when everything is going to shit, you need to know how to reach the plumber or the Poison Hotline without a minute to waste. (Side note – I think 70's parents would have made kickass Incident Responders. They totally get The Toilet Paper Principle.)

So here's another point I heard over and over again. Most Incident Response Plans have very clear escalation procedures and comms plans for everyone in the business who might need to be informed. Contact the CISO? Yep. Heads up to Legal that we've got an issue? Fer sher. Notify the leadership team? You betcha.

Well-defined Incident tiers, stratified by level of freak-outedness, as well as the contact requirements for each and the associated phone numbers? Those are all there in a good IR Plan. Many organizations, in other words, know exactly who they need to *notify* and how to reach them when there's a problem.

Where do a lot of them fall shorter, losing precious hours in the process? A lot of companies that are meticulous about how to reach VIPs simultaneously suck at giving equal attention to contact procedures for the workin' shmoes who can actually *solve the problem.*

For example, in large companies, it's not uncommon to have multiple clouds at different providers, plus company data centers, a Mulligan Stew of user devices on three or four different operating systems and so on. Pretty good odds that the guy who can solve a Linux problem in your Azure cloud and the guy who handles centralized management of company Android tablets ain't the same guy.

Likewise, and I may once again be stating the obvious here, but in bigger firms, cyber security personnel don't actually control, or even have access to, the environments where bad guys are likely to get in, poke around, and then break and/or steal stuff. The cyber team might have read-only access, or might just observe what goes on in those environments via the logs pushed into a SIEM. Even if the cyber team does know where the problem is, what the problem is, and how to mitigate the problem, they are likely *not* the ones with the access and permissions needed to *fix* the problem.

Depending on whether you need the MS Office guy, the mail server guy or the database guy, and whether the problem is in the data center, your Google cloud or your VOIP phone system, you're gonna need different someones. In other words, there's another list of people you might need to reach who are *not* the leaders and lawyers itemized in the IR Plan. Rather, they are the IT, Ops or engineering people who do real work in the world and may number in the dozens.

This is where that list by the phone comes in. In the age of smartphones, no one, not even my 70's era mom, can keep that many doctors, neighbors and emergency hotlines in their head. You need to have a list handy of not just who's-who but who-can-do-what. Keep it as up-to-date as you can, and (once again) keep it *on paper*.

And the "Mr. Yuk" sticker? Or its IR equivalent? Just like the green-faced icon that all of us of-a-certain-generation knew as kids, if you have nothing else written down, there's one number that should be, metaphorically speaking, stuck to the back of the handset where everyone can find it. It's the number to call in the Smokejumpers.

# 6.
# Smokejumpers

If you're not familiar, the term "smokejumper" is, in the literal sense, the nickname for the men and women who leap out of perfectly good airplanes, which already makes them total badasses, to parachute into giant raging forest fires. This obviously makes them even badassier badasses.

In Incident Response, the term has been adopted to mean the folks who jump in on short notice when something big and bad goes wrong enough to require calling in emergency outside help. The folks at these external firms are specialists. They do this all the time, and to the degree that anyone *can* be prepared without knowing your environment, your business processes, your network topology and so on, these are people who know what to do as soon as they get there. Like the guys with the parachutes and the pickaxes, they can hit the ground running.

Typically the firm they come from will be a specialty IR company or a consultancy that is hired on retainer. It may be a zero-dollar retainer, or it may be a many-dollar retainer, but usually it's some form of agreement that says they will have people on the phone and/or on-site within a certain number of hours when the retainer is invoked.

My view is that *any* company of significant size should already have an IR retainer in place. In perfect keeping with The Toilet Paper Principle, the day you need such a provider is not the day to start googling to locate one. You'll easily find them, but once you get them on the phone, you'll inevitably find they're fully booked for the month ahead.

By all means if you wish, keep the upfront cash outlay as small as possible, but try to have someone under contract in advance so they are ready to jump when you need them. Just remember that the smaller the retainer, the less snappy the response times, so plan your risk tolerance accordingly.

Here's another big thing to keep in mind. We've talked about how people go fuzzy-brain when things go bad, and the corresponding importance of clear processes. There should be absolutely zero confusion about *how* to get the fire-eaters onto the jump plane. It should be a documented, very quick process to invoke the retainer, i.e. what number to call, what email address to ping, etc. and it needs to be right there on Page 1 of Ye Olde Oh-Shit Binder like a big green Mr. Yuk sticker.

Second, smokejumpers ain't cheap, so it needs to be very clear who has the authority to make that call. Because the minute, and I mean the minute, these folks gear up and head to the metaphorical flight line with their parachutes, the meter is running and these are pros who may come in pairs, or dozens, depending on the level of oh-shitedness. And they can run thousands of dollars a day. Each.

So do the math on that. Even a pretty significant retainer of twenty, fifty, or a hundred grand can get eaten up very, very quickly. That retainer? In a significant Incident, the retainer is not what pays the bill for the work. No, dear friend. The retainer is just what ensures that they will actually show up to *start* the work. If you think the retainer amount will cover the engagement itself, you either haven't been through a major Incident before and/or you just haven't thought through the arithmetic.

So now you know who and what smokejumpers are. Here's the boil-down. Have a contract in place. Know who can invoke it. Know what the response SLAs are, that is, the service level agreements that guarantee how fast they are obligated to have someone on the phone, or in your office, and so on.

In keeping with The Toilet Paper Principle, you should also get very clear *before* the bad day happens what they will need, what they will expect, and what they will want access to when they walk in the door reeking of pine tar and wood smoke. Which brings me to my next point.

# 7.
# Where Are Your Keys?

If I had a nickel for every time I asked myself, "Now where did I put my keys?" I'd have... a lot of nickels. So here's another Incident Response Standard of Excellence to aspire to. Don't be like me when it comes to not having your keys.

In this case, I'm referring to API keys, and more generally to any means of access you or your smokejumpers might need during an Incident. RFID keys to the supply room? Old school metal keys to access parts of the physical plant? More generic use of the metaphor for passwords, accounts, AD groups and so on? Yep, all that stuff.

For a lot of good and understandable business reasons, when you bring in a new hire, getting their access provisioned, getting roles and permissions correct and so on may well involve a series of requests, approvals, service tickets and processes. None of this is a problem on a nice calm day. The new hire will need to pick out their dental plan, meet their colleagues and find the coffee pot, so what's the rush getting them all set up with tools and system access?

There is no time for that during a major Incident. Interviewing all those folks who'd learned stuff the hard way, I heard this point again and again. You should have a predefined set of API keys for the smokejumpers and their tools to access data, as well as any needed accounts, permissions, roles, Active Directory groups, and/or whatever other lingo applies to your specific environment. When the smokejumpers take your call and head for the jump plane, you want them to be able to get right to work the minute they land.

Obviously, the primary reason is to help fix the problem as quickly as possible. But you should also remember as I said in Chapter 6, the meter is running from the moment their boots hit the ground. Let's say you have just four rockstars parachuting into your crisis, and they work in pairs on 12-hour shifts, billing out at 300 bucks an hour. If they have to laze about playing Angry Birds on their phones while you try to get them the access they need, you can add nearly $15,000 a *day* to the cost of the Incident while nothing happens because you couldn't find your (API) keys. It's a bad look for everyone involved.

Now it might seem like I'm about to talk out both sides of my mouth here, but I'm not. It is also true that the principle of least privilege and good security practice in general mean that access to sensitive information, production environments, various sources of logs and so forth are and should be very tightly controlled. You don't normally just have keys, accounts or access, especially access to super secret-squirrel cyber stuff, lying around unused.

Indeed it is often the cyber security team that receives all the grumping and stink-eye for imposing exactly this type of basic discipline. Trust me, you haven't experienced indignance until you yank the wildly promiscuous permissions from the software engineer who was Employee #3 ten years ago, and is incensed when you take away his ability to push hot fixes into Prod from his home laptop.

So how do I reconcile the two points I just made?

*Me*: "You must have ready-made access to all the things, in a drawer, available on a moment's notice!"

*Also Me*: "Don't you dare get undisciplined and sloppy about accounts, roles, privileges and access! This is like cyber security 101! Bad dog! Hit yourself with a newspaper!"

The answer is two-fold. First, classic Toilet Paper Principle. When you sign up with your smokejumpers, or even assign in-house people whose role will change in a crisis, you should establish exactly what access, data sets, roles, groups and so on will be needed. Have a kickoff meeting, review the controls, study the network topology and such ahead of time, *not* when the building is already on fire. Then provision the necessary roles, accounts and so forth for generic Users like Smokejumper 1, Smokejumper 2, etc.

Yet it is also true that these accounts pose an enormous risk if not handled properly. If an outside actor were to compromise the environment and gain access to a dormant superhero account, they could potentially do a huge amount of damage to the business. As a result, it should go hand in hand with the creation of these accounts to create threat detections around any changes to or use of them.

If anyone is added to these groups, any addresses or names are changed, literally anything happens at all, this in and of itself should be treated as a Priority 1 Incident. It should trigger alerts, set off a klaxon and activate a big red blinky light. So yes, absolutely create these things; empty but ready to activate. Then lock them down with chains, three padlocks and a steel door, put cameras on the door, and wrap it all one of those laser-beam fence things you see in all the heist movies. And as for the door and the padlocks, please make sure you know where you left your keys.

# 8.
# How do you get to Carnegie Hall?

On the off chance you don't know this story, there's an old joke about a guy standing on a street corner in Manhattan with a map, holding it this way and that, clearly confused. Finally out of frustration he folds it up again, turns to a man coming down the street and says, "Excuse me, how do you get to Carnegie Hall?"

The man replies, "Practice, practice, practice."

So let's take stock of where we stand so far. We've talked about the importance of preparation. We've also talked about the limits thereof, since we've acknowledged that nothing is going to go the way we expect. In keeping with the Toilet Paper Principle, we've covered how and why to set up the basic infrastructure for dealing with the super-sucky day when it comes.

We've got the documents and the processes. We've written out what we shouldn't do, what we should do, and step-by-step guides for how to do all that stuff. We've set up the access and the accounts, and done prep work and knowledge transfer. The team has memorized the playbook, printed it on paper just-in-case, and is ready to step out on the field. It's time to start warm-ups, run a few drills and eventually shoot for a full-on scrimmage game. Here's a few tips for how to do that well.

**Rule #1 – Start small.** If operational exercises and testing of controls, people and processes is not already part of your business-as-usual, then start with a small, easy bite of the apple. Before you try to simulate an attack, coordinate across teams, or game out a big, hairy superbad day, go with something a few people can do in, let's say, an hour or less.

For example, you can run a drill on a single process. Grab a handful of people around the table.

Turn to one page with one SOP and say, "OK, you! Turn to page 26. Read the process shown there, try to step through it, and let's see if we hit any snags."

Whether you do this live at a keyboard, or just talk it out around the table will depend on exactly what it is you're trying to validate, but I think that distinction is actually not all that important. What matters more is the degree to which the activity reinforces your confidence that the process and the people are ready on this one specific point if today turns out to be that really bad day.

**Rule #2 – Make it a habit.** As much as you possibly can, make these efforts a regular part of your op tempo. I believe it's more important to run *regular* exercises than to run *big* exercises. A once-a-year, all-hands IT drill will undoubtedly produce key learnings and good takeaways, but it leaves as untested everything that didn't just happen to be covered in this year's exercise.

What I'm talking about is small things. Process walk-throughs. Little team-level tabletops. Start with quarterly, and aspire to every six weeks. When that pace feels well-practiced and sustainable, double it again. Work through more pieces, find more rough spots and smooth them out. Remember that every problem you discover and fix on a nice, calm, sunny day is one you won't have impeding your Response during a real Incident. During that Incident I will say again, people are going to be way more prone to mistakes, missteps and confusion because all the brains will be going, "Ahhh! Tiger!"

**Rule #3 – You're testing everything.** It's important to remember that every element of Incident Response - people, process, and technology - is subject to error, change and obsolescence. If you just switched your EDR solution to Crowdstrike and the procedures and screenshots from last year show how to isolate a host using SentinelOne, it's not going to be a lot of help when the drill commences. The *Process* may still be perfect. The *Procedure* will be useless.

Likewise you could have all your documents in perfect order, but a change in personnel means the people may be the weak spot. The universe has a sense of humor, so just assume that your Incident will happen on the one night that the on-call person is the new guy. If he came from a QRadar shop but you're running Splunk, better to spot the weakness in a dry run than when the red phone rings.

**Rule #4 – The method matters less than the discipline**. As you get better at this stuff, you can expand frequency, scale, scope and methods. You can run emulated attacks with some simple scripts or you can model known actors' TTPs with an Attack Simulation tool. You can run Red, Blue and Purple Team exercises, and so on.

Personally, I love tabletops. As a business guy, I like the ROI. They can be quick, they don't require the same investment as a live pentest or red team. Yet *never* have I run one, even a small one, that didn't surface at least a couple of concrete ways to improve.

The takeaway is that exercises, drills and tabletops, no matter how large or small, run regularly, will surface issues and help you keep everything – documents, systems and people – current with the environment. So practice, practice, practice.

# 9.
# Play the B Team

Here's another piece of advice I received from an anonymous contributor. Perhaps because the lessons they shared involved difficult situations or negative outcomes they couldn't openly talk about, they asked not to be named. I think their anonymity thus enhances, rather than detracts from, the weight of their advice.

One of the things they emphasized was that there is an exception to the old adage that, "how you practice is how you play." The exception is that sometimes, the folks who played at practice might not always be there to play on game day. So, as they put it to me, assemble your team, prepare the exercise, and then, like a backup quarterback playing exhibition before the regular season, "occasionally, send in the B-team." Let your second-string players, your less experienced employees or your newest team members play out the exercise, which almost by definition will be a pressure test of your Processes and Procedures. The less institutional or tribal knowledge the game players have, the more they will have to rely on what is actually written in the three-ring binder.

The reasoning is simple. If you design all your Plans, Processes and Procedures assuming that every major Incident will happen on a day when your A-team is available, you're not planning for reality. People get sick. People go on vacations and honeymoons. Sometimes, by sheer dumb luck, your best people won't be there when you will miss them the most.

If you want to go a step further, plan the exercise as usual but, in the spirit of what is now sometimes referred to as Chaos Engineering, pull a key player out of the exercise only at the last minute. Like, literally the last minute, just as the exercise begins. Walk into the meeting, put up the slide with the scenario, and only then remove your lead detection engineer, your IR Manager, or your best digital forensics expert to see how the team performs without them. Have your benched A-players watch. Have them take notes. Have them prepare feedback for their understudies or stand-ins.

The more you simulate real-world challenges, the more prepared you will be for what a truly bad day might bring. Give your second-string players time on the field. Let your B-team have a turn at the plate. Prepare for days when things don't go as expected, because as Von Moltke and Mike Tyson reminded us, when the crap starts flyin', reality rarely aligns with the ideal conditions under which the Plans, the Processes and the Procedures were written.

# 10. Two Cans and a String: Backup Communications

We covered earlier that the Plans, Processes and Procedures that I just alluded to should be documented thoroughly and written down, on actual paper, and kept in a drawer somewhere. It is entirely possible that the attack you are responding to may have taken down your network or otherwise made it impossible to access all that great stuff you worked so hard to create. None of that diligent effort can help you if the stuff only exists on a network or a device you can't reach.

This next and related point may seem obvious, but I would argue if it were entirely so, I wouldn't have heard it from so many of the people I talked to for this book. Your IR Plan should similarly include a backup communications option in case your e-mail, your instant messaging platform, your office phone system and so on are degraded or rendered unusable.

It is also possible, as one anonymous Responder put it to me, that those communication channels are not *unusable*, but they are *untrustworthy*. What if the evidence you already have raises the possibility that, as the old campfire story goes, the call is coming from inside the house? The threat actor could be in a compromised account or have other access, and could be surveilling those channels. I believe the interviewee's exact words were, "Ask me how I know?"

A different contributor described to me an Incident that kept dragging on because the attackers appeared to have a nearly supernatural ability to anticipate the company's next move and be ready to counter it. When they did finally beat the case into submission and all was known, it turned out that the adversary had gained access to several of the laptops *in* the conference room serving as the Incident Command Center. The bad guys had activated the microphones and were listening in on everything the defenders were planning. This kept them, with almost laughable ease, one step ahead of the company's efforts to defend itself.

So a really good IR Plan should account for the possibility that your normal comms could be rendered either unusable or untrustworthy by an attack. If that were to happen, how would you communicate?

The most common advice I heard was either a mobile messaging platform like WhatsApp (ugh) or Signal (better) or a standalone secondary conference call platform. For instance, if your primary channels are Microsoft Mail and Teams, someone in legal or BC/DR or crisis comms should have an unused but active Webex or Zoom account, ideally with all the needed prefabricated groups ready and waiting.

What groups will you need? I'd start with at least an Executive group, an IR group, an IT leadership group, plus a distinctly-labeled channel that includes counsel and Legal staff used only for privileged conversations. Everyone in those groups should know how to meet physically and virtually under emergency circumstances, independent of normal channels. Just like invoking your smokejumper contract, it should also be clear who knows how to, and who is authorized to, activate those fallback communication channels.

I'll close here with another of those golden nuggets I learned in the course of my interviews. I'm merging a couple of stories here, fuzzing the details for good reason, but take it as a parable. Let's say that as we just discussed, a company had an Incident that involved loss of normal comms. In line with the idea we just discussed, said company failed over to alternative channels. Contrary to what we just discussed, they did it in a haphazard and unplanned way.

In our anonymized fable here, the employees were passionately working to support customers. The technicians were fighting off the attackers. Everyone was on SMS, Gmail accounts and plain old landline phone calls, doing all they could to keep the business running by any means available. It was amazing that they managed to maintain the flow of information and continue operations despite the attack. We're talking freakin' hero stuff.

The ouchy footnote to the story with the epic themes and the Hans Zimmer soundtrack? Let's pretend for the sake of illustration this was a pretty big company. A publicly traded company. Let's also say for the purpose of our example, it was a pretty big breach, one that led to some pretty big losses. Which led to some pretty big litigation. Litigation, of course, means discovery.

Those critical communications, that thin thread by which these people heroically kept the lights on and the business moving? Yeah, that was all on the executive team's *personal* phones. Those devices, and *everything* on them, was later subject to discovery. I will leave to your imagination what might have been on all those phones, relevant to the case or not, and how excited all those driven, connected and/or powerful people were to hand over that little gizmo in their pocket to someone else's lawyer.

A final word on this topic, then. To test some IR processes at my company last year, I drove to the Best Buy six minutes from my house and bought a cheap Android burner phone. It was a few big steps behind the latest Google or Samsung handset. It was slow and underwhelming, but it could make calls, send texts, surf the web and play high-def video on a pretty big screen. Ten years earlier it would have been viewed as miraculous.

Including the phone, the SIM card and the first month of data, it was *fifty* bucks. Given the little story I just told you, I'd argue that even if you don't expect or can't get people to regularly carry two phones, keeping a few dozen in a drawer for a rainy day is more than worth the cost.

See you at Best Buy.

## Part II

# The Day Arrives

# 11.
# Who's in Charge?

So the theoretical bad day has arrived. You're in the early moments of a significant Incident. Before even worrying about the compromise, the Response process or the impact, there's a much more practical question that really must be addressed first.

Who's in charge?

After talking to those twenty-plus people I've told you about, as well as my own experience in IR, I think the best answer is two-fold.

First, at the end of the day, executive leadership runs the business and has to make the decisions about what best serves that business. At the same time, a major cyber Incident is likely going to entail a lot of system details, technical facets and competing potential responses which business leaders are not equipped to assess, analyze or choose between. So leadership needs to do what is best for the company, the customers and the investors, but someone needs to manage the case, limit the damage, and frame the decisions for those leaders to take.

Enter the Incident Commander, or IC.

There's a lot to cover here, so I've actually broken the conversation into two parts; This chapter will focus on the *role* of the IC, i.e. responsibilities, authorities and duties, and the breakpoints between the IC's role and that of business leadership. In the next chapter, I'll talk about what kind of *individual* is best equipped to succeed in that role. So let's start with the role itself, and how we carve out those distinctions.

**Authority and Governance** – I know, I know, "Authority and Governance" is dead sexy stuff, and you're probably all hot and bothered right now. Try to cool down though. This is actually kind of important.

In terms of authority for threat detection and analysis, technical assessment, *non*-disruptive containment and rapid response, my view is that the IC should be in tactical control. Isolating non-critical systems, blocking traffic, suspending accounts and the like? If the impact is not going to blow up the business, the IC should have full authority to act.

When response actions *do* pose a risk of material disruption to operations, and/or a risk of significant adverse outcomes later during the eradication and recovery phases, then the IC must serve as a strategic advisor. The IC needs to communicate in effective and non-technical, jargon-free terms. They need to frame decisions that must be taken by leadership, and if they have any, make recommendations about those decisions, supported by the best available information.

Leadership's role is far more complex. First, they must assess the information from the IC, and ask questions from a broader business perspective that the IC may lack. Then they have to make high-impact decisions about eradication, recovery and after-action activities that may have ripple effects on the business long after the immediate danger has passed.

The executives will have shareholder, customer and press issues to think about. There may be legal, regulatory and contractual disclosure requirements to be met. If a breach was involved, there may be privacy and partnership issues triggered by the technical compromise. So how do you draw the lines between where the IC is empowered, and where they are in an advisory role to the powers that be?

I'm a huge fan of the old adage that a problem well defined is half-solved. So at least to someone with my type of brain, a structured approach is hugely helpful here. One method shared with me, one I really like, is a decision-making matrix that helps to lay out clearly where the IC's authority stands on its own, and what must be escalated to business leadership. To be absolutely clear, I'm not saying the example below is right, it's for illustration. I've tried to genericize the concept here to get you thinking.

| Decision Type | Commander 's Role & Authority | Business Leaders' Role & Authority |
|---|---|---|
| Tactical Security Response (e.g., isolating compromised systems, blocking network traffic) | Incident Commander has full authority, within pre-defined IR playbooks | Not Applicable, as the IC is empowered to execute autonomously |
| Forensic and Technical Investigations | Determines scope and methodology | Can offer guidance, surface any constraints, but does not dictate |
| Containment & Remediation Actions | Full authority unless the action has the potential for material business impact (May benefit from an actual $/$$/$$$ matrix) | Leadership must authorize if decisions will materially impact customers, operations, revenue or shareholders |
| Customer, Media and Regulatory Communications | Provides factual input, technical support, but does not speak to any outside parties unless requested | Legal, PR, Crisis Comms and/or SLT own and control press, customer and/or regulatory disclosures and messaging |
| Financial and Legal Risk Assessment and Decision-Making | Serves as advisor and consultant, providing technical assessment and insights into possible business risk or impact analysis | SLT (GC, CEO, CFO) own all decision-making |
| Incident Closure and Lessons Learned | Leads technical review and documentation, reports summary to ELT, Board or others as directed | Business leadership integrates insights, improvements and key learnings into evolving Enterprise Risk Strategy |

This version is admittedly oversimplified and lacks detail. Thus, you will need to tailor it back to the particulars of your own company. At the core though, what this tries to make clear is that the IC is in charge of the technical response, but executive leadership remains accountable when an Incident involves high-level risk and business trade-offs.

**Decision and Escalation Thresholds** – Another tool I learned which I likewise appreciated was the structured use of "Decision Thresholds" that serve not only as rules of thumb under time pressure, but also as a clear defense later in the event of second-guessing by Monday morning quarterbacks like regulators or class-action attorneys.

The idea here is that the organization can establish predefined escalation cutoff points that determine when the IC must consult business leadership and when they are empowered to act autonomously. Note that for this approach to work effectively, it is dependent on exactly the type of clear definitions and good documentation (e.g. Incident Severity, escalation call trees, and so on) for which I advocated in the early part of this book.

So for instance, suppose we have defined four levels of severity for an Incident based on operational or customer impact, expected cost to the company, and so on. Then a threshold-based approach might say, for example, that there is a WAG or "Wild Ass Guess" level of cost that each severity level may incur. Based on that we can define authorities like this:

- **SEV-3 and SEV-4 incidents (low/medium impact)** ⇒ IC has full autonomy.
- **SEV-2 incidents (significant but contained impact)** ⇒ IC must notify the CISO, who updates executive leadership as needed, but the IC can act independently if in keeping with the *extant, documented* IR process, procedures and playbooks. *Other* actions must be approved by the CISO or other executive-level authority prior to execution.

- **SEV-1 incidents (major business disruption, dollar costs or compliance/regulatory impact)** → IC or CISO must brief the appropriate leaders and stakeholders, who will provide strategic decisions that will drive the tactical response.

Having this system in place ensures that leadership defines the guardrails as well as the escalation requirements when a case may require a broader business view that even a highly competent but technically-focused IC may lack. *Within* those guardrails, however, the IC is empowered to execute in defense of the business without undue bureaucracy or delay.

This approach prevents unnecessary executive interference in low-level incidents while ensuring leadership retains oversight and decision-making authority in cases with a significant potential impact on operations, shareholders or customers.

So now that we've talked (a little) about what an Incident Commander *does*, let's talk about who, at least ideally, an Incident Commander *is*.

# 12.
# What Makes a Great IC?

Now that we've talked about the *role* of the Incident Commander, let's talk about the person who actually has to fill that chair. If you're a higher-up leader, these are things to look for. If you yourself are the one with your ass on the hot-seat, these are things you can (and I myself try to at least) hope to achieve.

A quick note before we dive into the details. This question could be a book all by itself based on all the feedback I got, so keeping it to the approximate length of every other chapter was daunting. If you think I've missed a hundred points, I'm sure you're right. In the end, I have tried to distill all I have heard and learned into just a few pages. To do this, I've selected the small subset of facets I believe are the *most* important to who and what makes a great IC.

**A great IC is an outstanding communicator** – This is the basis of everything else the IC has to accomplish. The IC must be able to articulate status, problems and potentially tough choices to executive leadership. That all has to be effectively couched in the language of the business. Executives speak of customers and costs, revenue and risk, probabilities and outcomes. No one on the top floor gives a shit whether the attacker used Silver or Cobalt Strike for command-and-control, and you won't get any points for knowing the difference. The IC must have the skills to explain technical issues in a way that actually lands with key stakeholders, and they must frame issues and required decisions clearly to effectively inform and escalate upward.

A good IC must also be exceptionally effective at organizing and delegating downward. They must have the skills, the vocabulary and the *emotional* acumen to allocate resources, direct the investigative process, and manage teams of stressed out, overworked human beings in crisp, clear ways that keep a hundred balls in the air and keep people focused on the right things. We will cover all of these things further in the chapters ahead, but effective communication - clear, concise and authoritative - is the foundation stone on which everything else must rest.

**A great IC understands the tech** – To effectively delegate, allocate and manage downward, a great IC must obviously also have a strong technical understanding of various domains of IT and security. If the IC doesn't understand what the analysts and engineers are explaining, they cannot effectively lead or make decisions.

This does not mean they have to be a deep expert in every specialty. In fact that is probably unrealistic. An IC will have varying levels of knowledge in different domains of security, and that's OK. No one person is likely to know packet inspection, PCI reporting requirements, network architecture, log analysis and disk forensics all to the same level of depth. They have to understand *enough* to assign, manage and/or work with the people who *do* know those things deeply so that they can do their own job as outlined in the previous chapter.

**A great IC understands the business** – At the same time, a great IC needs to understand enough of the operation to put the attack, the damage, and the containment, response and recovery options in context for decision-makers. Yes, there may well be a leadership layer such as the CISO, CTO or CIO between the IC and the business executives. A great IC however, would still ideally have a solid understanding of critical business functions, the revenue chain and customer delivery. If the IC doesn't know the Minimum Operating Capability (MOC) required to get or keep the business running, they can't effectively frame the problems, options or risks for the folks upstairs, or advise on proper sequencing of recovery efforts.

**A great IC has the trust of those above and below** – Everything I just said is all true, though I would call it "necessary but not sufficient." By the time a big bad Incident arrives, ideally a great IC will have used their communication skills, their EQ, their knowledge of the business and their technical acumen to have built trust with both leaders above and practitioners below. Without trust, an IC simply *cannot* fulfill the role as we described it in the last chapter.

Leadership must trust that the sitreps, assessments and requests from the IC are the best available under difficult conditions of imperfect information. The analysts and engineers working the problem must trust that the IC is making the tough calls as wisely and thoughtfully as possible. And everyone must trust each other in an absolute shared commitment to getting out of the mess, together, with the IC at the technical helm. In the end it is trust, not the title or the role, that gives the IC the authority to act, and to wield the influence that ensures that all teams respond to the IC's commands with their absolute best.

**A great IC is highly disciplined** – This is true in a number of directions, all of them vital in their own way. In one sense, the IC should be extremely rigorous in terms of structured, clear and unemotional analysis. Using the business and technical knowledge we discussed, they should be able to process highly complex circumstances and come out with actions, tasks and resource allocations that are properly sequenced.

Likewise, they are also disciplined in the sense that they remain focused on the important, and successfully manage toward outcomes amidst a cacophony of the urgent, the noisy and the distracting. They know how to keep their eye on the ball, even as people are shouting, throwing things and running around with flailing arms like Kermit on The Muppet Show. They must retain the ability to remain both calm and focused in a crisis, to behave in a way that is urgent, yet methodical.

The reasons above are probably obvious, but partly because it's relevant and partly just because I thought it was wild when I heard it, I'll throw in one more reason you may not know. My research showed me hard evidence that fear and panic actually *are* contagious. Like, According to Science.™ It's too long to go into here, but imagine a bunch of people jammed into a conference room as the network is burning down, and all eyes turn to the Incident Commander for cues as to how bad it is and what to do.

Now go Google the keywords "Stonybrook Study, Fear Sweat." The ten-second version? They had people stick cotton pads in their armpits while they ran on a treadmill, then before skydiving for the first time. Then they had other subjects wearing brain sensors *smell* both sets of pads. The result? The sniffers were measurably freaked out by the skydiving pads, but not the ones from the gym. The point? Fear *is* contagious via our subconscious processing of our environment and the people around us. We started this entire book talking about what happens to Responders' brains when they think they're about to be eaten by a tiger. So no matter how worried they may be in their own heads, an outstanding IC will project calm authority during a crisis. Which brings me to my last point.

**A great IC is courageous** – Finally, being a great IC requires a dauntless soul. This is not hyperbole. While I absolutely would not contend that I myself have achieved this when it was my turn at the rudder, a *great* IC has genuine fortitude. Some reasons are obvious. Telling management that the crap just hit the fan isn't an easy or pleasant job. Dealing with a potential damaging or even "extinction-level" event for the organization is obviously intimidating to even the most experienced Responders. If you don't feel you need some level of courage to stand in this role on a truly bad day, you're either a sociopath or one of those lizardy sleestak people from Land of the Lost.

A great IC may also have to deliver very difficult messages to their own teams and to leadership. The job will require making hard decisions with far-reaching implications for the business, usually under conditions of frighteningly imperfect information and enormous time pressure. A great IC acknowledges unknowns. A great IC provides realistic, fact-based assessments of conditions without sugar coating. A great IC speaks truth to power.

To sum up then, a great IC is the paramount communicator, is technically credible, and has earned respect from those above, beside and below. Perhaps toughest of all, a great IC needs the chillaxing vibe of a buddhist monk, the brave heart of William Wallace and (regardless of gender) a pair of cue-AC/DC-soundtrack big brass bollocks. That may not be any of us, it certainly isn't me, but it's something we can all aspire to.

# 13.
# Know What Race You're In

Let me start this chapter by saying I absolutely understand that this may not be easy or entirely reliable to determine at the beginning. Nevertheless, at the outset of an Incident, to the degree it's possible you should try to figure out as early as you can, the answer to this question:

What kind of race are you in?

More specifically, to the best of your knowledge, do you think you're preparing for a sprint, a marathon, or a relay? Let me explain what I mean.

Suppose, to illustrate by example, you have what appears to be a bad-but-contained issue. For instance, you get an alert that triggers quarantining a single endpoint. Depending on the particulars of the machine and the user, this might constitute a hard, fast race to ensure containment, check for data loss, eradicate the problem quickly, and assess any damage. This scope would likely have little impact on the overall operations of a large enterprise. That's what I would call planning for a Sprint. Best guess? Assemble your needed players and focus on a speed run to the finish line. Your approach would thus reflect this type of expected race.

Contrast this with what I'm calling a marathon. Suppose, to lean on a well-publicized example, you get an alert that someone successfully deployed crypto-mining software on your public MoveIT server. MoveIT is essentially a glorified commercial version of an sFTP server. Attackers found an unpublished MoveIT vulnerability and exploited it globally in mid-2023.

If this initial alert was *all* I had to go on, I would begin planning for a potential marathon. Why? First, I've got a public facing asset that may be compromised, so I need to mitigate, remediate and restore that asset for the business. Before I restore, I need to know when and how they got in, whether they established persistence to stay inside, and if any of that affects the backup I would restore from. Then I need to know if they managed to move from that initial foothold elsewhere in the environment. That's one set of worries.

Here's another. Because MoveIT is for large file transfers to and from outside entities, I will need to assess whether the attacker got into not just the compute, but the data. If so, there will need to be a complete damage assessment on god-knows-what they might have seen or copied. What if that data is regulated? Now I have a breach, reporting requirements, and so on. And what if the data were *altered*? Could someone messing with the files cause operational disruptions, or god help us, a life-and-safety issue down the line? That's its own whole separate snake knot of problems.

Both these tracks will require management communication, possible invocation of smokejumper retainers, engagement with counsel, and possible notifications to various regulatory and oversight bodies. This will not be, can not be, a case of "all hands on deck till it's done and then we all go home to get some sleep." This set of activities may go on for weeks.

One of my favorite anecdotes about this type of Incident was shared with me by a colleague. "One of the smartest things I ever saw," he said, "was the first night of a major Incident. It felt like a big chunk of the entire company was jammed into our largest conference room. It was standing room only. The CEO pointed his arm down the center of the room. Then he waved it to one side of the long conference table and said, 'This is going to be a long haul. Half of you, go home. I'll need you in the morning.'"

I think you get my point. From staffing schedules to assessing single-threaded expertise on your team to care-and-feeding, you need to start planning from day one if you think you're in for a marathon.

Finally, this may be more rare, and perhaps I'm torturing a metaphor here, there could be what I will call a relay. A relay is where the initial assessment is that you're going to hand off the baton. I've certainly seen smaller or midsize organizations that may not have the in-house depth of bench to handle a long-haul Incident at all.

For example, in many smaller firms the security or even the IT team is so limited that the need to sustain their day jobs means there just aren't the skills, the bandwidth or the number of hands needed to carry the water involved. In these cases, the strategy may be to simply package up everything that is known and hand it off to someone else like your smokejumper firm.

In a larger enterprise, this approach might simply be more strategically beneficial. In other words, taking the internal IT or cyber folks off their day jobs may be so disruptive to operations or strategic projects that it's just better or cheaper to zip up the whole mess and dump it in someone else's lap.

In a relay, the internal teams' primary focus will likely be to document everything that they know, and then hand off the case to someone else. After that, a common dictum is "with regard to the stuff involved in the Incident, stand back and don't touch anything. For everything else, everybody go back to work." This is vitally important both so the internal folks get back to running the shop, and so they don't interfere with or scramble the logs or investigative processes on the affected assets.

A relay situation therefore has different implications for how you need to plan around your people, your procedures, and what you prioritize. So to end where I began this chapter, suffice it to say that you should try to gauge what kind of race you're in. It will help you to figure out how to navigate the rest of the Incident Response lifecycle. So take your best guess and plan accordingly. Next, let's talk about exactly how to do that.

# 14.
# Care and Feeding

Now that we've talked about knowing what kind of race you're in, let's get into the details of leveraging that knowledge effectively. We talked earlier about human capacity under stress. If you're pretty sure this is a marathon, then as I said, there is a whole range of support activities you need to address that may not be required for a short, all-out sprint.

Taking care of this stuff is not going to happen by itself. As soon as you decide this is likely to be a long race, I'd suggest you do this. Designate someone to provide for care and feeding and the other needs of a stressed, overworked and soon-to-be-exhausted team. Note that I said, "to provide for || the care || and feeding || and other needs..."

I was being very specific, so let's take those in order.

**To Provide For** – You need to create a method to actually *provide* all the stuff below. IR works like everything else in business. Nothing. Happens. Without. Money. So before we talk about all the stuff you'll need to pay for, don't overlook that you'll need a *way* to pay for it.

This might seem simple. "We'll just use someone's corporate card." I'd say to that, make sure you know who that someone is, how to get hold of them in a crisis, and who to grab if they're not available. I'd also make sure that they have no, or at least a very generous, spending limit on that company card. Simple example - with people working all day and night, let's say you need to plan for meals four times a day. Let's also say you've got a total of 20 people, 12 hours on and 12 off, so ten mouths to feed at any given one of those four times each day. Let's do that math at, say 15 bucks a pop? Just the monthly meal bill is $*18,000.*

If possible, I'd suggest a distinct cost center, reserve account or budget line for IR or crisis expenses. Hang it up on the balance sheet as a reserve in January, and if you don't need it, finance can sweep it up on New Year's Eve and put it back into the profit line. (If that's Greek to you, just ask your accounting team. They'll totally get it.)

You may also want to check whether you need a policy exception documented for rapid procurement, invoicing or immediate payment for things that exceed what can normally go on a P-Card, or for providers who don't take card payment. If possible, set this all up ahead of time of course.

**Care** – With the fate of your business possibly on the line, you will need your team at the very best they can be. While food may be the most obvious need (see "feeding" shortly below), there are a host of other things you'll need to take care of. Here are a few.

- *Hydration*: This one is easy to overlook. Make sure there is an endless supply of water and other healthy beverages available 24x7. Like stress, lack in this area measurably degrades performance, so keep people well hydrated.

- *Bathing*: If your team is centralized in a SOC, office building or other company facility, start thinking about hygiene on Day One. There are many reasons for this. One is that bathing, showering, and hygiene routines can help people feel refreshed and energized. Routines also reduce all those "Ahhh! A tiger!" chemicals we talked about in Chapter 1. Some (crazy and/or badass) people use a cold shower to wake up. Others use a warm shower to reduce mental and physical tension. If your building has gym or bathing facilities, arrange unlimited access until the Incident is over. If not, try to arrange an alternative such as at a nearby hotel or fitness center.

- *Supplies*: Provide a ready stock of personal hygiene products from toothbrushes to deodorant to shampoo. I shouldn't have to say it, but please make sure that includes products specific to your female team members. People who feel better work better, so provide for these human needs. Making sure these materials are present can also send a clear message that you are *thinking about* their human needs, so they don't have to.

- *Exercise*: Here's another reason to make arrangements with your on-site or nearby gym or workout space. Some people need exercise to unwind, to get going, or to feel and operate at their best. Don't make figuring this out one more thing they have to take time and cycles to do. Do it for them. You need them wholly focused on saving your ass.

- *Relaxation*: In addition to an actual workout or gym space elsewhere, you may want to look at creating a quiet, restful space where team members can briefly decompress. Yoga mats, pillows, dim lighting and even the right music can provide relief for short breaks while still on-shift.

**Feeding** – A statement that is always true but even more so when you need your team at their very best; Ask any elite athlete about this. High performers need to be *nourished*, not just fed. Also, though we rarely think about this, many people across the teams you're relying on have dietary restrictions, religious beliefs, medical conditions and personal preferences around food.

So to explain my stance on the "feeding" part of care-and-feeding, I'll share a quote I loved from a former big company IR guy. "Pizza is for the after-party." My face must have looked kind of "huh?" so he explained. "Listen, I love pizza. But for me, pizza is reward food. It's cheese and fat and grease and a ton of carbs that puts me in a freakin' coma. It's not nourishment, it's celebration."

He did not, and likewise I do not, mean this as a finger-waggly admonition. Rather, it's shorthand for a more generalized concept. If this is a marathon race, you can't just whip out the corporate credit card, order a dozen pizzas every six hours, and expect people to soldier on day and night for weeks.

The body and brain are highly sensitive to what is in the gut. The stress response also triggers automatic deprioritization of digestion. Processing your last cheeseburger, which (if you didn't know) normally takes 2-4 days, isn't a priority when that tiger is chasing you. Thus, even though you're entirely unaware of the change, mother nature pretty much puts digestion on slow-roll during freakout mode. This is why stress leads to all manner of gastrointestinal problems.

The same is true for other stuff that's not related to surviving the next two minutes and climbing a tree, including *your immune system.* In other words, on top of all your other problems, your people are at greatly increased risk of getting sick right when you need them the most. It's going to be tough enough. Don't make it worse by offering only processed garbage bereft of actual nutrition. It *will* affect performance.

Don't try to dictate what "good" is, either. Each individual knows what food they prefer, what energizes them, what comforts them, and what they need in terms of nutrition to operate at their best. Logistically getting them those things may mean ordering from a dozen places instead of one, or essentially catering large diverse menus, multiple times a day. It may mean having a full-time team of gophers running meals. (More on this in the chapter about Good Help.) Accept this and get someone assigned to make it happen.

The cost and hassle of keeping your team well nourished, and therefore more healthy, more mentally sharp and more able to slog through long hours, may be significant. On the other hand, it is trivial compared to what a loss of analytical ability or good judgment could cost you because Andy the Analyst is on his 17th consecutive meal of vending machine crap.

**Other Needs** – There are going to be other things people need as well, too many to itemize here, so I will just close by proposing that you apply the same principles discussed here. Have a way to pay for what they need, then get it for them, and from the get-go make this someone's job, not an afterthought. Make it someone who's *not* a technical expert you also need on the Response, and empower them to make stuff happen for the people on the front lines.

A final thought. We haven't talked about sleep yet, and that's intentional. Sleep, and not just getting sleep, but *making and defending the time for* sleep is a critical responsibility for both the human-needs coordinator and the Incident Commander. For this reason, it gets its very own chapter, one that fully half my interviewees named as a Top-Three priority of all their lessons learned. Onward...

# 15.
# Incident Response Zombies

So let's talk about sleep. In a large enterprise, the cost of system downtime can run into the millions of dollars per day, or even per hour. This means that the stakes in a long-duration Incident could conceivably be as high as the survival or failure of the business. As such, there is going to be enormous pressure on IT, cyber security, and every other involved team to solve the problem as fast as possible.

This ties back once again to estimating quickly what kind of race you're in. If the answer, unfortunate as it may be, is that you're in a marathon not a sprint, then the CISO, the Incident Commander, and other functional leaders must resist unsustainable pressure from above and protect the down time built into the schedule for key personnel. In the battle against the cyber attackers, these people are your front line badass warriors, and even badass warriors need to rest. You know who says so? The badass warriors.

One study, "Fatigue Effects in Military Operational Environments" published by the U.S. Army Research Institute of Environmental Medicine documents how chronic sleep restriction leads to declines in "general cognition, problem-solving, and decision-making." I'm not a doctor or anything, but those sound a lot like the stuff I've been arguing are kind of important in high-stakes Incident Response.

Lest you remain unconvinced, here's another one. There was a paper presented at the Military Health System Research Symposium in 2024. It found that after a relatively short number of days, the combat effectiveness of warfighters who get only four hours of sleep a night vs. a "normal" 7+ hours per night, can drop by up to eighty-five percent.

Eighty. Five. Percent.

That's not "a few points around the margins" or "a performance tradeoff" to be made. The U.S. military, aka the folks with what is now approaching a *trillion*-dollar annual budget, did the research and they say that, quite quickly, inadequate rest turns even elite soldiers into bumbling zombies.

This same theme has been validated again and again in other professions. One landmark study, "The Impact of Sleep Deprivation on Surgeons' Performance" strongly demonstrated that exhaustion leads to a significant increase in errors. Increased errors sounds pretty bad to me, but on the other hand, they're only surgeons, so it's probably fine.

I'd love to be a fly on the wall for those conversations.

"Doctor, you left a sponge in my thorax!"

"So? What's your problem? I mean, free sponge. Geez, some people."

It's not just doctors either. More studies, same outcomes. First responders? Yep. Emergency personnel. Check. Oh, also? Air Traffic

Controllers. Pretty much any industry that the Department of Labor files under "jobs where effing up gets people killed" has run a study on the superbad effects of being bone-tired. Spoiler Alert - they all say the same things. Exhausted people make mistakes, some of them disastrous.

So now let's go back to my hypothetical scenario. You're in the midst of a long-duration Incident and the team is looking at weeks of all-out effort to help the business recover. The executives, the regulators, the press, and my italian mother-in-law are all screaming "I don't care if you have to work 100 hours without sleep, just fix it!" The problem with that, as I hope I have convincingly argued, is that pushing people to keep going beyond the point of diminishing returns is dramatically, demonstrably, documentedly, a terrible idea.

No one is going to want to hear that message, by the way. One more reason (again) for the points made in Chapter 12. The Incident Commander or CISO has to know what they're doing, has to have the credibility to stand up to pressure and be listened to, and should resist dangerous demands to cut corners. If you're in a prolonged, high-pressure Incident, it's critical to schedule and safeguard adequate rest time for the teams working the problem. Protecting these rest periods is essential to maintain performance and reduce the risk of errors that could *worsen* rather than resolve the problem.

I know this is way easier said than done, but if it looks like you're in it for the long haul, then the IC needs to defend the team's rest schedule with tooth and claw. If you yourself are the IC and anyone tries to run roughshod over you on this, just send them links to the studies I mentioned, and then ask them how they'd feel about a sponge getting all gooey and infecty in their thorax.

# 16.
# Get Off the Phone!

So you've declared an Incident, you've got a bead on what you're up against, and you've got someone making plans to take care of the many people you will need. More often than not, the next, or parallel, step, is to get those many people you will need on the phone.

Not surprisingly, every person I talked to has had the experience of being on conference calls during an Incident that had 20 or 50 or in one case (no kidding) 300 people on the line at once. And proving that irony is the most powerful force in the universe, the colleague who was once on that bridge with 300 people? <Insert his bitter laugh, even now, years later> Yeah. Per Chapter 5, none of those people were either of the two guys who could actually fix the problem.

Which brings me to the point of this chapter. Earlier in this book we talked about having the information ahead of time that you will need to get the right people on the phone. Here's an interesting corollary to that. There are at least four separate reasons to make sure that if there's anyone you *don't* need on each call, get them *off* the phone as quickly as possible.

The first and most obvious is this. Every person dialing into that bridge has work they were doing before the oh-shit bell rang. Even when jumping in with the best of intentions, every person on that call has a day job. And every one of them will be not-doing that day job if they are sitting on a conference bridge listening to, talking about, or freaking out about a problem for which they can't actually provide any help.

By definition, this will impact normal business operations. I mean, if Sally and Freddo and 20 of their friends can sit on a bridge doing nothing for hours on end and it *doesn't* impact normal operations, they probably shouldn't be working there in the first place. So if people can't help, then in the interest of the business, get them off the damn phone and back to their day jobs. The best thing they can do for the business is keep it running as close to normally as possible while the right SMEs work the problem.

Second, if an Incident kicks off during a normal work day, you may have multiples of the same skill set, e.g. two security architects, joining the initial call. To put it in nerd terms, over the course of the Incident, you may need them serially more than you need them in parallel. In this case you should get one of them off the call because you don't want to burn them both up at the same time, when what you really need is one available on each shift in the days ahead. Like the CEO with his arm down the middle of the room in Chapter 13, let some of them go home so they can rotate through the role over time.

The third reason is that in some cases, the folks joining the call will be business partners or contractors or consultants who are not actually company employees. If there's anyone on the call that gets paid by the hour, the cost is irrelevant *if they can help*. If they can help resolve a major issue, then they're cheap at twice the price, regardless of their price.

On the other hand, if they *can't* help with the Incident, get them off the phone because they're just adding to the cost of the Incident while adding no value. Most by-the-hour folks will be perfectly happy to sit there with no ability to help, no responsibilities, and the meter running. Over the course of my career, I've worked with AT&T and Verizon and most of the big consulting firms, and every one of those people has an annual billing target. If you let six of them sit on a call accomplishing nothing, contributing nothing, and doing nothing except billing by the minute, trust me, they will.

Reason number four is my personal favorite. Regardless of the particulars, the nature or the severity of the Incident, it is generally true that being in the middle of oh-shit is not a good thing. At least in many cases, it may reflect some control or process failure, and/or it may portend a potentially material impact on the business. As such, especially in a publicly traded or highly regulated company, the nature and details of that Incident may be the subject of compliance reporting, possible litigation or other downstream effects later on.

In anticipation of any of those scenarios, the fewer people who know the details of the Incident the better. Anybody who is not need-to-know, well, doesn't need to know. Anyone who gets to stay on the phone should have a role to play in resolving the Incident or a role to play in managing and dealing with the fallout from the Incident. Anybody who doesn't fall into one of those two categories should be shooed out of the physical or virtual room as soon as possible.

There's an old adage in the intelligence community that the likelihood of sensitive information being compromised is directly proportional to the *square* of the number of people who know about it. It is nonlinear. So minimize the likelihood of leaks and maximize your control over sensitive and possibly damaging information by limiting those who *do* know to those who *need to* know.

I'm sure there are more reasons that I'm forgetting, but those four should be more than enough to make the point. To keep the business running as close to normally as possible, to make sure you have people available for the long haul, to keep the hourly-rate leeches from bleeding you dry, and most of all to keep the sensitive details as close to the vest as you can, assess everyone you don't need to be there, then get them the hell off the phone.

# 17.
# Keep Your Tab Open

This Chapter is unique because it's built around something that came up with just one of the two dozen people I interviewed. In some ways that made it all the more intriguing as something that falls into the "often overlooked" aspects of IR that was the premise for this book. Also, lest you think I'm just regurgitating whatever I heard, good or otherwise, I can say as the MBA bean-counter in the room that I'm pretty confident this is really good advice.

So she said to me, "make sure that somebody's keeping a running tally of costs as the Incident goes on." She noted that it won't be perfect, in fact it will be wildly imperfect. Other departments from Crisis Comms to Property Management will incur costs for everything from running the office HVAC 24x7 to needing more cleaning shifts to take out all the extra trash. So you won't know half of the costs, but it's important to do it anyway. Track what you know and let the accountants square it all away later. Just do your part to log what you spend or see yourself.

Some of the costs, like the food, rest and wellness expenses we just talked about will be small dollars in the grand scheme of things. Some others, like the lawyers, consultants and smokejumpers will be...bigger. Total costs will also stretch across teams, budgets and departments. No matter. Keep a tab, and either write down, or task someone else to write down whatever you note as you go.

So that's the what-to-do. What's the why-to-do-it? One reason is that some of your costs may be within the scope of your company's cyber insurance. Management is incented to try and recoup every nickel they can after the Incident has been sorted. Insurance companies are likewise incented to contest every documented expense, but you can be darn sure they won't pay a penny for undocumented ones.

Second, even if the only people who ever see the tally are internal, there are all kinds of "managerial accounting" or equally nerdy reasons why having these costs detailed as accurately as possible will be important. This is especially true in a publicly traded company, where disclosures about the Incident and tallying up the total cost to shareholders is absolutely going to be a point that someone is going to care about later. (I worked for Price Waterhouse back in the day. The CPA weenies live for stuff like this.)

Finally, and this may seem cynical if not outright manipulative, but I don't think it is. It is in some sense a form of strategic thinking. In the vein of, "never waste a good crisis" I have seen it happen where an Incident can accelerate or serve as a forcing function for the organization to make changes to the environment, the controls or the network that were already planned for some future date, or had been raised as needed, but not funded.

Let's say you were planning to swap your endpoint protections next year from one EDR product to another but the business decided to kick the can down the road a year or two to save a little money because an inferior product was cheaper. If you just had a big issue with malware getting all over User endpoints because your current EDR failed, the business might want to accelerate that to "right effin' now, please."

In addition to actually improving your endpoint protection (which was the reason you were going to do it anyway) another driver *could* be that if you do it RFN, the costs can be shoved into the bar bill for the Incident. In other words, some management teams might say, "well if we're gonna take the hit anyway, let's pile some directly-related changes and improvements into the cost for the breach. We'll lump it all in there, take a one-time hit on the next earnings call, and move on."

If management can push through some accelerated security upgrades as part of the cost of the Incident, things that would otherwise have hit the IT or cyber team's budget next year, it may actually free up budget dollars for other things you wanted to do but didn't have the money for. So next year, the money that was for that thing can now be spent on an *additional* thing. Woot!

As I said, this may seem cynical, but if there's a way to make lemonade out of lemons from a resources standpoint, that absolutely should not be overlooked. For any cyber team with a constrained or insufficient budget, which in my experience describes *all* of them, this may just be the one silver lining. If a major issue ultimately results in a net increase in resources to better secure the environment, that's a beneficial outcome. So keep a tab, and keep it open.

# 18.

# Write it Down! (But very, very carefully.)

As you organize resources, divide up shifts and assign roles, here's another thing to think about. Your Incident Commander will need a scribe. A note-taker. Someone who can capture next actions, due-outs and owners.

It can't be any ol' schmuck walking by. It needs to be someone who understands enough of what's happening and the terminology to be effective at listening to and curating the live discussion and taking effective notes. At the same time, it is unlikely to be one of your core IR team or necessary SMEs. You're going to need those folks, your Incident Responders, your IT admins and other key players, to actually work the problem.

I can't tell you who the right person is in your own organization. Based on what I said above though, I could suggest that you start with someone who is in cyber or IT but who is *not* in a role that can assist with the issue at hand. They need to be off the critical path for resolution of the crisis, but have enough knowledge to understand what's happening and be willing and able to help.

To illustrate by example, you might have a compliance analyst who deals with cyber-related frameworks and regulatory requirements like NIST-800 or PCI, but whose skills aren't the ones needed to actually put out this particular fire. They likely speak the lingo, and may well know the IT, cyber and Legal teams involved during the Incident, but are in a realm adjacent to, rather than central to, the Response.

Another example might be someone from cyber, but from a domain that is more "left of bang" than "right of bang." For example, while your SOC analysts, threat hunters or detection engineers are likely to be fully engaged, you might have a security architect or other resource whose day job is more focused on the preventative aspects of security. They too would be likely to have the knowledge, lexicon and desire to assist. Let them.

Also, you will likely need more than one. Like every other role, if meetings, updates and investigative reviews are happening across more than one shift or time zone, someone will have to be taking *clear* and *concise* notes as you go. Notice by the way that I did not use the words *comprehensive* or *exhaustive* in that last sentence. Which brings me to another of my absolute favorite hadn't-thought-of-that's from researching this book, one of those, "oh, that's the voice of painful experience right there" things.

After talking to a couple of folks with the scars to support this admonition, my advice is to *not* use the exploding crop of automated note-takers and dictation tools available on all the major conferencing platforms. Even if most of your Responders and cyber SMEs are all in one place, it's almost certain that your Management updates, coordination with vendors and partners, and other cross-functional sync-ups with Legal, Corporate Comms and so on will be on Zoom, Microsoft Teams or some other conferencing platform. I would strongly suggest you *not* rely on their auto-transcripterator doodads. Here's why.

Some of these conference bridges will remain open for hours, or even days. There may be vigorous discussion, disagreement, evaluation of competing options, and decision-making that involves difficult tradeoffs. Weighing and choosing between unattractive options often involves verbally "playing the devil's advocate" or itemizing various bad outcomes, not to mention revealing who as individuals are advocating for and against which choices, with or without appropriate humanity, sensitivity or awareness of future consequences.

So do you really want a robotic scrivener running in the background taking down every word, good or bad, heartfelt or heartless? For any number of reasons, but I'll itemize just three here, my take is you do *not* want all of that stuff committed to paper.

One reason is that if the various stakeholders on these calls know every discussion, every hypothetical, indeed every word they utter is being transcribed, it could very well have a chilling effect on what may *need* to be a vigorous and contentious discussion to get to the best outcome. Simply put, if people are afraid to speak up because the tape recorder is running, you could end up with a less ideal outcome than in an environment of healthy debate.

Second, suppose the SOP says, "when the Incident is over, and all the after-action stuff is completed, our written policy is after 60 days, all call recordings not in litigation-hold are deleted." It is, one could imagine, possible that this process is not automatic, and someone might forget. And should said someone forget, the recordings are going to be discoverable during the litigation that may well follow months or years after a major breach, which you may prefer to avoid. Lawyers gonna lawyer, you know what I'm sayin'?

The last is slightly less obvious. Even if you're totally comfortable with every word that was uttered by every person on every call, many companies do not have ultra-fine-grained controls over who has access to the Teams folder, Sharepoint drive or whatever system you're using to store the audio and text when they're done. Which also means that, even inadvertently, you could have people with no need to know anything stumble across Incident details, thanks to a keyword search meant to find photos from the ugly-christmas-sweater contest.

My personal take on do's and don'ts for what goes into the official record?

**Do's:**

**Key Decisions:** Document decisions that were explicitly made or agreed to, including the rationale for each if it's straightforward and uncontroversial, e.g. "after discussing various options, there was consensus that we will do X because it represents the best option for reasons Y." Depending on duration of the Incident, this could apply to each shift or call, or this could be in a scribe's one output for the whole Incident if the case all fits in a single outbrief.

**Action Items:** Clearly record next steps, due-outs, assigned owners, and deadlines for all Action Items agreed to during the call, shift, or conversations covered by the write-up.

**Timeline of Key Events:** Log a factual, chronological timeline of major actions, events, and milestones during the Incident or since the last update, e.g. additional investigative steps undertaken or new findings discovered and their impact on the status of Operations and/or the Response effort.

**Outbound Communications**: Capture summaries of information shared or reports sent to leadership, counsel, or external stakeholders such as customers, regulators, or partners.

**Critical Notes for Post-Incident Review**: If there are things that aren't a priority now but will be important later, e.g. an update to SOPs based on gaps found during the Incident, log a quick note as a reminder for formal exploration later. Stuff for the After Action Report (see Chapter 26, Persistence Hunters) or long-term process improvements should not take cycles and attention away from the immediate firefighting, but there may be many and they are easy to forget days or weeks later when the fire is out. Take a brief note to remind you later, then put a pin in it until you're out of the woods.

**Don'ts**:

**Speculative Discussions**: As we discussed, sometimes a battle of ideas and vigorous debate is healthy, even vital, but I would generally avoid putting any hypothetical scenarios, unverified theories, or "devil's advocate" arguments into the official log of events or outbound updates.

**Conflicts and Opinions**: Leave out emotionally charged exchanges or views that could be misinterpreted later. Everyone will be under a lot of pressure, short of sleep, and suffering all the cognitive and emotional impacts we discussed earlier that are tied to our brain's fear of being eaten by a tiger. Document the disagreements only insofar as they are factually necessary, e.g. in order to frame an explicit decision between conflicting options for Management to arbitrate.

**Confidential or Privileged Information**: It goes without saying, but don't write down any sensitive or regulated data in the log, e.g. mask credit card numbers, anonymize PII and so on. A bit less obvious is to avoid logging particulars that could expose sensitive business or legal information like unreported financials, secret research efforts or pending M&A deals in a document that may later be subject to discovery or found by someone you didn't intend.

To sum up, then, keeping good records is obviously a critical part of the IR process. What I hope you take from this chapter is that the definition of "good" includes the wisdom to know what does and doesn't belong in the official record that will endure long after the case is over.

# 19.
# Postcards to Leadership

So here's another step in the IR lifecycle that actually *is* covered in some manuals and training courses. The step in question is when and how you communicate to business leadership that there is, or may be, a serious issue, and how you update them thereafter. In my view, the problem is that those IR manuals and courses are understandably written by security experts. As a business guy first and a security guy second, I think they miss some key points when it comes to talking to the business.

Let's frame the problem. Suppose at some point after an alert goes off, the Tier 1 SOC does initial triage and escalates to the Tier 2 or CIRT team. That team in turn says, "Yeeaah… sooooo, we think this might actually be a thing." At this point, there's some line in the See-Chapter-2 documentation that says someone in cyber will need to let someone higher up in and/or outside the cyber food chain know that there might be, or definitely is, a thing. Doing that well is an art unto itself.

I should note here that although this *shouldn't* be true, there may be some fear for many folks in being the bearer, even the innocent bearer, of bad tidings. Upon hearing of Antony's betrothal to another woman for example, Shakespeare's tells us that Cleopatra threatened the poor schmuck who brought the news with, "the unhairing of his head, whipping him with wire, stewing him in brine and and then smarting him in lingering pickle." Boy, nothing says "being the messenger is a dangerous job" like being flayed and dipped in vinegar, amiright?

But let's suppose that you are indeed the one to whom this unfortunate duty falls on our hypothetical bad day. How do you do it well? For what it's worth, I've taught my teams a practice I call sending a postcard.

This method is simple, and sending postcards to leadership should follow a clear set of rules. This approach both helps ensure the message is effective, and it also nicely adheres to the earlier discussion about clear procedures being a welcome support in times of high stress. If you must be the one to do it, telling leadership it's Oh-Shit-Day is something you want to do right. Here are the key points.

1. **BLUF first**: I try to state the bottom line up front (BLUF). Capable business leaders process information and understand implications very quickly. Don't bury the lede. Get to the point first, then provide the minimum necessary context. Most important of all is this - if there is a decision that needs to be taken at the leadership level, set that out in the BLUF, with the supporting details in the body of the message.

2. **Brevity**: Keep it short; aspire to keep your initial notice or recurring status update to something you could fit on a postcard. Where they need more information, they'll ask.

3. **Consistency**: These should follow a consistent format. Don't just use this for the initial notification. As much as possible, have your SitRep template follow the same pattern. This

trains the recipients that what they may want to focus on will always be in the same place. Remember, they're under pressure too, so make their lives easier where you can.

4. **Cadence**: Set a clear expectation for updates, e.g. "A SitRep will be provided every four hours or upon a material change in findings until the Incident is closed." This will provide preemptive assurance to executives that if they haven't heard from you, there is nothing new that is important enough to leapfrog the established comms schedule. This keeps them calm and your phone quiet so you can focus on actually doing the job.

5. **Essential Information Only**: You can make one that suits you, but template the process like everything else so it's ready to go and easy to use when people are in freakout mode. Here's my basic starter list if you want an example:

    - *Incident Overview*: Provide a concise summary of the breach, compromise or issue, including the nature of the threat (e.g., malware, unauthorized access), and any known systems or data impacted.

    - *Potential Impacts*: What, if anything you know so far, about possible effects on Operations, payment flows, or other processes that matter to the people who manage the business of the business.

    - *Detection Timing and Reliability*: Specify in a few plain-English words how and when the Incident was detected. Technical details aren't important, the keys are when the issue was discovered, when (if you know yet) it actually happened, and how reliable the assessment is at this stage. In other words, is this a "just in case" heads-up, a for-certain crisis, or something in between.

- *Actions Taken*: Outline any investigative steps already completed and what they have found, and containment or mitigation steps already implemented to prevent further damage, if applicable.

- *Next Steps for Cyber/IT*: Outline what steps are still to follow on the investigative and technical side.

- *Business/Leadership Actions or Decisions Required*: If there is a decision to be made or action needed "above your pay grade" as they say, state the request clearly in more detail than is present in the BLUF. Provide necessary context, and if you have a recommendation, state and defend it in as few words as possible. Your job is to *equip* leadership to make the best decision they can with the imperfect information available. Leadership's job is to decide.

Having spent the rest of this chapter on things to do, I also want to close with a few things not to do. Here are the things I would try to avoid:

1. *Speculation*: Avoid unverified details or assumptions that are unsupported by data about the Incident's origin, scope, or impact. If you're right, that will be reported when it's more certain at a future update. If you're wrong, you've shot your credibility in the foot with the people who need to trust your judgement. State what you know, state what you don't yet know if that's relevant. Do. Not. Guess.

2. *Geek Speak*: This is absolutely not the time to try and impress anyone with how smart you are. Use clear, non-technical language in your updates to ensure comprehension by all potential stakeholders and recipients. The questions leadership likely cares about right now are, in roughly this order:

    - What's happening?
    - In what ways, and how badly, could this hurt us?
    - What are you doing about it?
    - How soon will it be fixed?

3. *Assigning Fault or Blame*: Finally, even if the Incident is directly linked to some threat, risk or unaddressed concern you've been shouting about for years, now is not the time for I-told-ya-so's. When there is a serious issue for the business going on, this is "one team, one fight" time. There will be time for a rigorous, objective and fact-based Root Cause Analysis later. While the fire is still burning, focus on getting out of the muck, not how and why you got into it. For now, don't fix the blame, fix the problem.

# 20.
# The Changing of the Guard

If you ever find yourself in London on a Monday, Wednesday, Friday or Sunday morning, I highly recommend you catch the changing of the guard at Buckingham Palace. The current ceremony, which dates back to 1837, is simultaneously impressively choreographed and charmingly anachronistic.

Now I assume that during a crisis your IR team will not be clad in bright red tunics and foot-high bearskin hats, though if they were that would certainly lighten the mood a bit. However, they too will need a way to transition from one team to another at the turning of the watch. For any Incident that's going to go on longer than a couple of days, you will either have to have breaks in the action, which the business will absolutely not want, or you will need to have people working in shifts. Some will work while some will rest and so forth.

As an Incident is worked in each eight-hour or half-day shift or whatever other arrangement you choose, new information will be discovered. There will be successful forward movement, but there will also be dead ends and dry holes, lines of inquiry explored and discarded. Capturing the work that didn't pan out is as important as noting the progress that *was* made so that efforts are not duplicated.

Without a structured way to hand off between shifts, teams or analysts, there is no safeguard that good-but-wrong ideas won't get re-explored, and time and resources wasted. Higher up the ranks, as it were, it is also absolutely vital that any communications made outward or upward, e.g. to business leadership, outside counsel or law enforcement, are properly captured and documented.

So there has to be a system of record. One of the key functions of that system of record must be an explicit way to do knowledge handoff between shifts or teams. Imagine for example that Freddo the Analyst is chasing some line of inquiry, let's say digging through application logs to try and determine the exact scope of a server compromise. And let's suppose that this takes longer than you can safely push Freddo in a single sitting without him turning into a sleepwalking ball of blurred vision and bad analysis.

At some point Freddo's gonna have to get some sleep, and someone else is going to need to take over where he left off. So even if it's a spreadsheet, a OneNote file, or a yellow pad and a pencil, make sure there is one source of truth for what work has been done, what efforts are in flight, and what is planned next. (Please also keep in mind the previous few chapters when you ponder what does, and doesn't, appropriately belong actually written down in this system of record.)

Distilling the net-out of an inquiry, summarizing any findings already communicated, and in general teeing up the next person to pick up where the first one left off is not administrivia. It is a critical part of ensuring an effective and sustainable Response effort. This may need to be repeated, around the clock, for days or weeks or months. There are a variety of ways to do this, including the ideas listed below, but the key takeaway is please make sure that you have a way to do it, some way to do it, *any* way to do it, and then do it consistently. If you're stuck for ideas, here are a few options.

1. Systems designed for this: If you have one, your SIEM, your SOAR platform or other security tool may have a built-in case management system, ticket-tracking or secure "war room" function designed to meet this need. If you're not sure, ask your technical contact at the provider or vendor.

2. Non-security tools designed for case or service management: If you don't have a security specific tool that is well suited, see if you have a ticketing platform (e.g. ServiceNow), task tracking tool (e.g. JIRA), a wiki or knowledge tool (e.g. Confluence) or, failing all else, a dedicated Teams or Slack channel.

3. In the event you don't have a great technical platform to manage all this in any form, then as part of the "Get Your Docs in a Row" concept, I suggest you make up a simple handoff template that is used at each change of the watch. Create a Microsoft Word or Google document for this purpose, and then save them in a folder after every shift with a common naming convention. This should capture in a few words key items like *Current Status, New Findings, Tasks Completed, Open Items, Escalations or Pending Approvals, and prioritized Next Actions.*

4. Finally, whether you are using a fancy SIEM or a yellow pad to capture that Handoff Status, I suggest an Agile-standup style meeting between arriving and departing teams. Ten minutes max, just enough time to highlight blockers, tasks to be completed, owners and deadlines. Keep it short and on point, and then get the departing team out the door and home to bed ASAP.

# 21.
# Gophers, Runners, and the Uses of Good Help

During a significant Incident that looks like it may last for quite a while there are going to be people who want to help. Some will be from adjacent disciplines, some from across the larger organization. There may even be family members from the team who want to be of help, but who can't assist directly in response, containment, and recovery.

These people represent a store of goodwill and potential good help. If you think back to our discussion about preparing for care and feeding you should be able to see where I'm going with this. Yes, Incident Response may partly depend on the folks who can analyze malware or update a firewall. Here's the thing though. To keep those folks at their desks when you need them most, some of them may need a prescription picked up before the pharmacy closes, or a ride to catch the last train home, or someone to feed their cat.

If you have people who don't know *how* to help, but *want* to help… accept! Take advantage of their offer and their desire to be of service in a tough time. These people show their true colors, and it's worth noting who they are, and the way they stepped up, for future reference when the crisis is over. In the meantime, make a list of all the things that you or your team might need from a gopher, a helper, or any trusted colleague with a driver's license.

For all the technical stuff that only the nerds can do, there are things you might lose their cycles to that could be handed off to the less-vital-but-willing. If you've been tracking all the prior sections on scheduling, nutrition, hygiene and caring for your team, you understand by now that there are a hundred things outside the keyboard that are required to keep the team in the fight.

So, just like you would with all the technical steps that need doing, start making lists, assigning tasks, allocating resources, and delegating. Find that coalition of the willing and put them to work. You're going to need all the good help you can get.

# 22.
# Uncle Charlie and the Turducken: The Dangers of Bad Help

So let's contrast "good help" with "bad help." So you know when your Uncle Charlie comes over for Thanksgiving and is just adamant that you haven't lived until you've tried deep-fried turducken? No? Maybe that's just a me thing, but let's just pretend for a second that my Uncle Charlie is your Uncle Charlie.

I suppose, just in case you don't know, that I should explain exactly what is a deep-fried turducken. It is basically the most profoundly absurd food item since the deep-fried, bacon-wrapped twinkie. (Yes, I hear you judging me. No, I don't care.)

So - you buy and debone a small chicken. Then you buy and debone a large duck. Then you buy a really large turkey. Then you make Thanksgiving stuffing out of, you know, stuffing stuff. Then you stuff the stuffing, *not*, as you might expect, into the turkey, but into the chicken. Then you stuff the chicken into the duck. If it won't go, you grease it with butter. (More on this later when it catches on fire.)

Then you stuff the duck into the turkey. What's great about this step by the way is that it inadvertently guarantees that you don't leave the plastic bag of giblets inside the turkey. This in turn avoids the possibility that they could be overlooked, resulting in a bird full of toxic chemicals and melted plastic, thereby ruining Thanksgiving for everyone, which could otherwise theoretically happen. Ask me how I know.

Anyway, back to Uncle Charlie. So he stuffs the stuffing in the chicken and the chicken in the duck and the duck in the turkey. Next, he sets up the engine hoist from his garage over the old oil drum he swears he cleaned "right good" before placing it over a kerosene heater and blasting it til it reaches the boiling point of peanut oil. In *your* driveway.

All of this has happened, mind you, prior to the moment you are brought into the story. He's just now rung your doorbell so you can enjoy, "the best part!" He's gonna drop that butter-lubed, triple-stuffed nesting doll into a cauldron of bubbling fat. "Lay out the side dishes, cuz in 4-minutes-per-pound-from-now, you're gonna have the best Thanksgiving ever!!"

Now let's suppose, just for funsies, that in his enthusiasm for the project, Uncle Charlie forgot to grab a towel and *dry* the turkey before he lowered it like a Chevy small block into the spattering hellmouth. If you're not familiar with what happens when you place *wet* turkey skin into nine thousand degree peanut oil, allow me to explain.

There will be an instant cloud of flying, gyrating misted fat particles, some of which will, without fail, find their way into the jet-engine paint-dryer that Charlie put under the pot to power the whole enterprise. When that happens, you will, inevitably and with shocking alacrity, end up with a raging fire fanning outward toward all nearby people, places and things. If you would like to see how not-far-fetched this is, just search youtube for "turducken fire." Hilarious.

I mean, except for all the terror and property damage. But except for that? Hilarious.

All of this would be just funny and/or tragic except for one thing, which brings us at last to what in God's name this has to do with Incident Response. This is the point in our story when Uncle Charlie, who, in his desire to wow you with his mad turducken skills, has waited far too long before finally screaming, "Fire!" When he does, your cousin who was peeling the green beans, in total ignorance but with the best of intentions, grabs a big pot of water off the stove and runs pell-mell out to the driveway.

Do you have any idea what happens when you throw *water* on a raging grease fire?

And herein lies the moral of our story. Good help, as we discussed, runs errands and walks dogs. Bad help does really dangerous things because it doesn't know any better. Like your cousin with the water bucket, people who think they have the right answer are going to want "help." Do. Not. Let them.

As we discussed in "Who's in Charge?" it is true that, ultimately, it is the business leaders who must decide on a macro course of action. But those decisions must be taken through the lens of the best possible *informed* assessment of cost, dollars and risk. Making sure that those decisions are indeed well-informed will require clear framing, ideally by the CISO, CTO or an outstanding Incident Commander of the type we discussed. Leadership's decisions must be made *inside of,* not *independent* of, the technical context of what is happening and the risks of each course of action.

If anyone - leaders, lawyers or laymen - offers their ideas for how to proceed, but *they don't understand what's happening or the potential downstream consequences of their suggestions,* stand firm. While ideas are welcome, the authority of the IC on the technical aspects of the Response is paramount. Worse still, if they charge out of the elevator and start Godzilla-stomping on everyone and demanding that they do dumb things and cut corners the risks of which they don't understand, then very kindly, respectfully, and with great tact, tell them to sit down and shut the fuck up.

If they need something to keep them occupied while you actually do the job, give them the emails stolen from the Sony Pictures breach. It will make very clear what an uninformed and ill-conceived executive response to an attack looks like, and how much trouble - legal, financial and otherwise - they could *personally* end up in if they continue to push for action on well-meaning but unfortunately-stupid ideas.

# Part III

# It's Over. Now What?

# Part III

# 23.
# Persistence Hunters

Welcome to the "after the storm" section of our funny little book here. You've made it through our archetypal crisis. Your business has survived. So now, let's talk about antelope.

Once upon a time, our collective ancestors roamed across the plains of East Africa. And because of science people doing science things, we have archaeological evidence that one of the things they ate was various types of gazelle and antelope. This poses an interesting quandary. Many of these critters are among the fastest land animals on earth. They can burst up to 40 miles an hour and maintain a sustained speed of 30 plus.

Compare this to the fastest human runners of today. Even equipped with the best technology Nike can jam into a $500 pair of shoes, the most elite marathoners on earth, many of whom still hail from those same parts of East Africa, can sustain about a 12 mile an hour pace. For more realistic mortals, let's call it 6-10 mph. So how does a 10 mile-an-hour caveman hunt down a 30 mile-an-hour antelope?

The answer is that back in the stone-tool days, we were biologically adapted for, accustomed to, and capable of, incredible feats of endurance. To use the technical term, we are designed by evolution as "persistence hunters." A 10 mile-an-hour caveman can indeed rundown a 30 mile-an-hour antelope because ol' Thog in the loincloth over there can keep that pace up for 10 or 20 or 30 miles and the antelope can't. The poor thing will eventually keel over, and if it doesn't die on its own of exhaustion, our buddy with the flint spear will take care of the rest.

In our modern world, we might consider this type of endurance entirely extinct except for an ultra-rarefied cadre of olympic athletes. Turns out however that we'd be wrong. To this day, for example, there is a tribe of indigenous people living in the caves of Mexico called the Tarahumara. These folks love nothing more than to get sloppy on fermented corn mush and go bounding through the mountains over uneven terrain for a 50 mile jaunt.

Generally well-fed and comfortable by the way, they don't even do this to wear down an exhausted plate of venison. Nope. Actually, it's often done as a contest. And what, you might understandably ask, is the prize for running two back to back marathons in floppy handmade sandals? They mostly do it just for funsies and bragging rights, with the occasional kiss from the hunter-gatherer prom queen. That's just their jam. In their own language, the tribe's name actually means "the running people." (If this all sounds absurd, check out "Born to Run" by Chris McDougal. I'm not making this stuff up.)

Aside from the fact that I'm a total science nerd, and my sense from my 25 years in this business is that a lot of other cyber people are science nerds too, the reason I include this little archaeological aside is this. Once the Incident itself is contained or cleaned up, that's not the same as "done." There is still a series of action steps that absolutely must be part of the closeout process. These constitute the difference between "resolved" which applies to the immediate issue, and "closed" which applies to the broader case as a whole.

The first of these action steps is sometimes referred to as a quick-n-dirty or a hot wash. I would describe this as an informal gathering to capture key learnings and takeaways while recollection is fresh. This is just grist for the later mill. Then there should be a formal After Action Report (AAR) in the days that follow. These reports are well defined and there are good examples available online if you don't have one. The military is a great source for examples. Here in the US, both the Army and Marines have a rigorous and long-standing discipline of completing an AAR to memorialize key learnings, identify process improvements, and understand leadership and tactical failures. Fully half the people I spoke to cited writing the AAR and then *actually doing the things in it* as a top must-do item.

Somewhere in that AAR, typically toward the end, will be a set of recommendations, action items, and due-outs. And this is where your persistence hunter comes in. Find the person on the team whose personality makes you think, "yeah, in the old days this would be the guy who would run down a gazelle for 27 frickin' miles." When it comes to making sure due-outs get done, that's your guy.

Put *that* person in charge of seeing that the hard-won recommendations remain tracked and on everybody's radar until they get done, or until someone with a fancy title and a big paycheck has put their name in writing saying, "Nah, we're not gonna do that." This may seem self-evident but just in case you're not pickin' up what I'm puttin' down, here are a few of the reasons so many people said that someone needs to own the due-outs, someone who will never, ever let those things drop.

First, these lessons have come with a huge price tag of financial, emotional, physiological and organizational pain. On some purely karmic level, it would pile insult on top of injury to do nothing with lessons earned at such a dear cost.

Second, sooner or later, someone inside the business but who wasn't directly involved in the Incident, e.g. compliance, investor relations, or corporate audit is going to come around at some point and ask, "So hey, that big terrible thing that happened. What did we learn? What are we doing about it?" Now imagine that your answer is, "Well, we wrote down a list of failures and improvements at the end of the Incident a few months ago, but we haven't really done anything with it." Probably not gonna be a great meeting for you.

Third, as you may have noticed me bringing up before, I come to the possibility, if not the explicit likelihood, of litigious, governmental or regulatory inquiries after the fact. If the Incident was big and bad enough, someone from *outside* the business like government inspectors or class action attorneys are gonna come sniffin' around asking questions. What mistakes were made, they will ask. Was the Incident properly handled? What are the consequences for shareholders, and so on. In my experience, sometimes these people may have no blessed idea what they're talking about when it comes to cyber security, but that can sadly be irrelevant in the real world. Given this may take a long time to materialize, it's an even worse look if you *still* haven't addressed the failures, oversights and stuff-we-can-do-betters that you wrote down a year ago when it was happening.

For all these reasons, you need someone to take point on tracking those changes and improvements to completion. And that person needs to be the most determined, persistent, gazelle-chasin' MF you can find. With all the new problems and crises and vicissitudes of life that will continue to crop up every day after the Big Hairy Incident is over, if the hanging chads aren't assigned to a specific, named individual, they're not gettin' done. *Someone* needs to be absolutely relentless in making sure those takeaways are run down until they are good and dead.

# 24.
# The "Rest" of the Story

So we're out of the woods, and you've put someone in charge of running down your key takeaways. There are still, as the title of this book puts it, some often-overlooked aspects to the human side of Incident Response. Once an Incident is over, your team will require time and support to recover from a drawn-out, all-out effort. (So will you by the way, so apply this to yourself when you can.) Chronic stress, high stakes, and long hours are not something you just bounce back from with a good night's sleep.

So how can you help your people decompress, recalibrate, and regain balance after enduring a prolonged high-stress mission? I got a *ton* of feedback on this, it was one of the two or three topics where I heard from nearly every contributor. Here's what they had to say on getting your team back in top form when the storm has passed.

The first thing you absolutely must make happen is down time, pure and simple. People need time to rest and recuperate. The kind of chronic stress a long Incident can incur can lead to serious physiological depletion. I'm not just talking about being tired or feeling worn out here. Being under constant, company-threatening stress can lead to all kinds of serious issues; adrenal exhaustion, digestive problems, insomnia and more.

So let's start with compensatory time off, or "comp time" as it is known. There are a number of ways to approach this. One option is a ratio, e.g. "for every hour above and beyond your normal schedule" there is some amount of time granted for comp time. Another is a step function like, "for Incidents of X length, it's a week off, for greater than that, it's two."

However you do the math, be more than fair and this absolutely should *not* be charged as PTO or "cost" the employee. This is recognition for going above and beyond. It's a show of gratitude, giving them back time they spent saving your ass from even worse outcomes. Make it happen. It's right and it's fair, and also remember that people vote with their feet. If their thanks for wearing themselves out, missing their families and working til they drop is parsimonious, you should expect their entirely justified response to be roughly, "Good luck with the next one, y'all. I'm out."

Here's one tip I heard several times that seemed obvious *after* I heard it. While you shouldn't dictate this, encourage your folks to take their comp time in a single block, or no more than two, and soon. Even if you gave them, let's say, two full weeks, i.e. ten business days, taking a day off here and a day there doesn't actually accomplish what this is about. They might think "Friday's off for all of July and August" sounds good on paper, but it won't actually help with the biological rejuvenation and health recovery that's needed post-Incident. They need to get *away* from work for a while.

As a side benefit, it is also much clearer and easier to handle from a managerial standpoint when you need to make sure that you have people on hand to watch your back while potentially your entire IR team is on a beach somewhere sipping margaritas. This is actually a thing in its own right, which is why we'll come back to it in about three minutes in the next chapter, "Cover your Asse(t)s."

Next, leverage any offerings, providers or infrastructure already in place. Many organizations offer Employee Assistance Programs, workshops, hotlines or other on-demand benefits for mental health, wellness and stress management. These may not be explicitly meant for, but are totally suited to, post-Incident recovery. If you're an Incident Response leader, coordinate with HR to understand all extant options and programs. Then, make sure that as soon as the hot wash is over, your team knows where and how to access these useful resources as you send them off to the aforementioned beach.

There are also more physically-focused health options that may be covered, either by existing health insurance, or by other options such as HSAs, flex spending accounts or wellness benefits. Whether it is massage, chiropractic treatments or other modalities, try to get clear on what may be available under existing coverage and make sure your team knows about it. This is, by the way, a perfect example of the kind of thing you can delegate to the "good help" we talked about in Chapter 21. If a colleague with zero cyber chops asks, "how can I help" during the Incident, try sending them on a mission to figure all this out so your answers are ready to go as soon as the fire is out.

For unusually long or intense Incidents, you should also look into partnerships with wellness providers or access to a wider range of services and resources, even if they aren't covered by insurance or fit into the "traditional" definition of healthcare. I had one long-time Responder swear to me that a combination of red light treatment (whatever that is) and yoga cut his personal Return-to-Operations

(RTO) time in *half.* Whether it's meditation classes or acupuncture, think of it just like our discussion on nutrition. Don't judge what *you* think is right or useful. Within reason, get your people what *they* say they need to get back in the saddle.

Don't think of this as "after the fact" but as an integral late-stage part of the wind down of the Incident itself. Consider it part and parcel of the larger effort. Any costs for these recovery enhancements quite rightly belong on the "Incident bar tab" we discussed in Chapter 17. A major Incident that went on for weeks has likely cost the organization six or seven or eight figures. Don't get stingy on the smaller costs when it comes time to say thank you to the people who saved your butt.

One more thought here, one that is very personal to me. While it was not Incident driven, I myself suffered a complete stress-driven health breakdown in 2018. I worked (and worried) until my immune system collapsed. I went septic, and ended up with an infection in my heart, which had then had to be *cut open.* As a result of this, I was supposed to be on a wide range of medications for the rest of my life. Six months later, I was off everything, permanently. How'd that happen?

A daily meditation practice, breath work and a complete change in my diet. You heard that right. Me, the spreadsheet-loving, anti-woo-woo MBA went from heavily medicated to heavily meditated, and the latter, not the former, made open heart surgery kind of a nothing-burger in the long run.

What's my point? If you are a leader, please, I beg you, on this one point… Lead. This is not the time for a prove-how-tough-you-are competition. Talk about the stress of what your team has dealt with. Tell your people that it's OK not to be OK. Acknowledge the realities of the need for rest, for wellness, for *joy.* Then make sure they know you have their back when it comes to getting those things. The one thing that most effectively crushes the flood of cortisol and stress hormones that destroy our immune systems and our health? Oxytocin. The only places to get it? Love, friendship, gratitude and rest.

One last thing, as small as this may seem. Some people (myself included as it turns out - thanks Hogan Personality Profile) are driven more by the desire to help than by money or fame. So say thank you, and know that saying thank you still matters. Tell your team how much you appreciate them, and everything they left on the field for you. Then send them home to hug their kids, kiss their partner, snuggle their cat and play with their dog. The science on this is clear. There literally is no better medicine.

# 25.
# Cover Your Asse(t)s

Now here is an unfortunate but mathematically true reality. Despite everything I just said about comp time, recovery, and taking care of your people, there is absolutely nothing that says you could not have another related or unrelated Incident shortly after you close the theoretical case we've been talking about. The result is that you absolutely do need to give people the break we discussed, but you also have to maintain adequate coverage in the event of another Incident.

How do you reconcile these conflicting demands?

I have certainly been talked through more than one case where a team wrapped up and put a bow on something they thought was done, only to realize that there was still an adversary foothold in the network. The industry is likewise rife with tales of restoring from backups only to discover the backups were compromised, restarting the entire crisis.

So how do you give people the break they need, the break they have more-than-earned, without leaving the company's proverbial trousers around its proverbial ankles? I believe there are a number of viable options.

You could, for example, consider keeping some of your smokejumpers around. This has several benefits. First, you can entirely-appropriately tack the cost of keeping them engaged onto the existing Incident while your own team is granted their rest and recovery time. To pure cyber nerds this may sound like financial housekeeping but I assure you it isn't. Who pays, where the money comes from, and how it's all accounted for are not insignificant concerns, they are vitally important.

There's a second benefit to this approach. Unlike bringing in someone fresh, smokejumpers who have just worked an Incident in your environment should have some familiarity with your controls, your monitoring systems, your SIEM, the network topology, the people involved, etc. Though on an hourly basis they are expensive, the time you would pay someone new to get up to speed on everything you just paid the parachutists to learn would almost certainly offset the lower hourly rate. So, put it on the tab (see Chapter 17 again) and keep them around if that's the right option.

A second option is to see if there are people in your team's professional network who might have the knowledge to make them an acceptable short-term stand-in. For example, (he says because he's seen it happen) someone might know an old friend or colleague who is not familiar with the environment, but who understands the current tech stack. A phone call might go something like this. "Hi <blank>. I know you've never set foot in my current company, but you worked with me in a previous job where the SIEM, firewalls and endpoint package were all the same as the tools we're using over here. Any chance I could pay you to come in for a few weeks to just watch the glass and call me if anything scary goes 'ding' for a while?" If you're old enough (like me…ouch) and have a good network, this approach might well get some takers.

Another option might be to call on a retiree or former team member from the current company who has moved on, but who might still know a decent amount about the people, the controls, the network, and the environment. They might also have their heart in the right place to support their old company or colleagues.

Last and probably least appealing but still an option, is to reach out to a Managed Services or specialty provider and pay the admittedly-absurd rates they would charge for a one-off engagement. This rate may sting a bit, but I would argue it's still a better answer than sending your worn out and emotionally exhausted team back right into their normal work schedule. In fact, my two cents is that doing that to your existing team simply is not viable.

At the end of the day these options will all still cost money, and not pocket change at that. During a major Incident, for better or worse, the checkbook is going to be open. So my advice to your management team is to willingly, even gratefully, accept that these costs are part of the total bill for the Incident, despite the fact that chronologically speaking, the Incident itself may be "over" in the eyes of the business.

Regardless of *which* solution you bring to the table to address the problem, you will need to bring *a* solution to address the problem. Your people are going to need their downtime. Ensuring that your asses, and your assets, are covered while they get that downtime should be considered an inherent part of the process, the costs and the methodology for dealing with and closing out a significant Incident.

# Conclusion – Winding Up (and Upward)

At this point we have, at least for the sake of my theoretical arguments here, reached the end of the Incident Response process, including all the after-action discussions, objectives, and activities. So I'll leave you with an image and a corresponding thought that I hope will tie together all of the overlooked, underappreciated and other practices shared with me for this book.

To say it again, I don't think what we've covered here replaces or supplants any of the traditional wisdom, published texts or expert guidance on handling the technical aspect of Incident Response. Rather, I hope this book has filled in some of the gaps that are missing from them.

I also hope by now I have made the same simple case that my Professor made all those years ago with his roll of toilet paper. My theory is that you will deal with a very bad day a lot better by not waiting until it arrives to think about it.

- By preparing policies, plans, processes and procedures *before* you desperately need them;
- By documenting who to contact for various needs so they are easy to reach when it matters;
- By knowing what skills and tools are available and to whom;

- By knowing when and how to reach out to outside experts, and who can and should do that;
- By developing challenging scenarios and practicing them regularly;
- By ensuring that you rest, feed, water and care for your warriors in every way they need both during and after the crisis; and
- By capturing learnings and takeaways to identify the gaps in everything experienced or emulated;

Your team should become better and better prepared for when a truly bad day arrives.

When that day does arrive, I believe that the guidance in this funny little book can also help to maximize the endurance, the cognitive abilities, and most of all the well-being of the people who you are trusting to get you through a major Incident. Taken together, the preparation for, the simulation of, and the response to, Incident after Incident (whether real or imaginary) should ultimately lead to a somewhat paradoxical outcome.

One of the contributors to this book, that crazy Responder-CISO-Pilot-Policeman I mentioned way back in Chapter 1, explained it to me this way. The more you embrace The Toilet Paper Principle, the less important it becomes. As you capture key learnings, close gaps, improve procedures, tune controls, add defenses, and communicate more effectively, in other words as you complete the entire set of necessary activities outlined here, then over time, the more cases you work the better you get.

Bottom line? If you keep striving to do it right, to fix what you learn, and then iterate, something strange should happen. The more you handle major issues, the less you'll need to. With every upward spiral you complete by addressing issues and then closing gaps, the fewer and smaller the future Incidents you should have over time.

At the end of the day, for all the technology on the cyber battlefield, this is a very human business. Perhaps even more so on its worst days. My genuine wish is that you never need any of what is in this book. If you do though, I hope that what so many people so kindly shared with me will help you to respond with more confidence, thoroughness, and care for your people than would have been true otherwise.

Good luck.

# Acknowledgements

No one does something like this alone, so I'd like to offer my deepest thanks to my wife Cathy, my biggest cheerleader, and KB, the best editor, best advisor and best best friend a guy could ever have.

As to the security-related content, I mentioned in the introduction, this book is not really mine at all. Rather, I am the scribe who simply tried to share in my own voice the wisdom and hard-won lessons of many people far smarter than I.

With that in mind, but also with an eye toward security, I'd like to express my deepest and heartfelt thanks to Nick, Tim, Keith, Lauren, Chris, Caleb, Andrew, Tony, Tig, Anna, Ash, Jonathan, James, Other-Tony, Brian and the dozen others who understandably chose not to be named at all. Whether named here or not, you know who you are and I cannot thank you enough.

# About the Author

Eric Olson is a cybersecurity leader with over 25 years of experience at the intersection of business and threat defense. Currently serving as Director of Cyber Security at a US Airline, he has led Threat Intel, Incident Response, Engineering and Product Development across startups, Fortune 500s, and government contractors. With an MBA from Georgetown and deep field time in the trenches of cyber defense, he brings business clarity to chaotic moments. This is his first book — written not for fame, but for the Responders who show up when everything goes wrong.

Made in the USA
Monee, IL
19 August 2025

22556234R00075